HOW TO BECOME A RECRUITER IN JAPAN:

The Ultimate Guide

www.mishayurchenko.me

© 2018 Misha Yurchenko

All rights reserved. No portion of this book may be reproduced in any form without permission from the publisher, except as permitted by U.S. copyright law.

BONUS MATERIAL

As a special gift to all my readers I've created a free PDF of 127 resources for your job search. It's a list that I wish I had several years ago when I was first interviewing -- it would have made things a lot easier.

The PDF includes resume templates, time management tools, and apps to supercharge your job search.

Please visit here to download the PDF:

https://mishayurchenko.me/free-pdfs/

TABLE OF CONTENTS

1. Introduction: Why Recruitment?........................ 1
2. Chapter 1: The Recruitment Model Explained 18
3. Chapter 2: The Japanese Market................................ 32
4. Chapter 3: How to Select the Right Company 45
5. Chapter 4: Landing the Interview 55
6. Chapter 5: The Interview Process.................................. 62
7. Chapter 6: How to Nail the Role Play Interviews 91
8. Chapter 7: Tips for Success 110
9. Chapter 8: Offers and Salary Negotiation................... 117
10. Chapter 9: How to Make the Best Decision.............. 131
11. Chapter 10: Voices from Recruiters 146
12. Conclusion 153
13. Tools and Resources 155

INTRODUCTION

It's extremely satisfying to watch someone join a company, build a product, and launch it to the masses. It gets my blood rushing to see a company turn their business around because of one person they hired. The "growth" part of this is all very motivating for me personally.

Of course, I didn't realize this until after I became a recruiter. If someone had told me that it could be this exciting or rewarding, I probably would have jumped on board sooner.

Like most people, the whole job-search process was usually always a black box for me.

I didn't really understand how to find a job, the best way to interview, or how to make a positive impression. I read books, sure, but it only went so far. For the most part, I had no idea what I was doing, especially when it came to finding a job in Japan. I luckily landed a job in the recruitment industry and had a chance to meet with thousands of job seekers and dozens of CEOs. This really opened things up for me.

I gained a lot of perspective into how companies hire and what they really value. I also got a lot of great experience helping people navigate—the job-search process. I realized that there's a pretty big gap between what job seekers are looking for and what companies are looking for. Employers and job applicants often approach the employment process from completely different perspectives, which often inadvertently results in various problems such as, hiring mistakes, miscommunications, and employee frustration.

I've spent 4 years in recruitment, but, like anyone who has worked in the industry for some time will attest, recruitment years are like dog years — you multiply them by 7. Like a lot of successful people in the industry, I kind of just "fell into" it. Was it my dream job? Did I want to do it for the rest of my life? No, but it was a lot of fun, I learned a heck of a lot, and I'm very grateful for all of the people I've met and the skills I've picked up along the way.

I believe a career in recruitment, whether that's internal, agency, or otherwise, can be extremely fulfilling. Japan has one of the most interesting and unique recruitment markets in the world, and is full of opportunity for those who are both starting out in their career or have several years of work experience.

Why should you consider a career in recruitment?

Recruitment teaches you real business skills that are transferable to virtually any industry. Sales, marketing, business development, writing, customer support, contract negotiation, relationship building, research, online marketing, networking, and so much more. Many recruiters I know have gone on to start their own business, others have joined big name companies like Google, Expedia, American Express, Amazon, and Facebook, and while most of them continued to do recruitment ("internal" recruitment), some of them moved into a different function likes sales or account management that's not specifically hiring related.

Indeed, a strong background in HR can set you up to be a CEO. Learning how to hire people is one of the most valuable skills you can gain and it translates to any industry. Ask any CEO, or senior manager for that matter, what their biggest challenge is at the moment. Nine out of ten times, they will say "hiring."

You can build an amazing network and gain access to people whom you would never, *ever* meet otherwise. CEOs and hiring managers want to talk to *you*. Why? Because you are helping them solve their biggest problem — hiring key individuals who are critical to the survival and growth of their company. In fact, the relationships and networks developed often extend beyond work; many of the friends I have today have been past candidates and clients with whom I've worked closely. When you take a real interest in getting to know the people you are dealing with in order to solve their problems, you build real trust and real human connections.

Selling something tangible is tough already, but selling something intangible is even more challenging. In recruitment, you're not selling something; you're selling some*one*, which adds another layer of complexity (and responsibility!). If you can master this (or even if you can gain a decent level of proficiency) then you'll learn how to persuade, influence, and gain trust from people. You'll see their confidence in you grow as you build these relationships.

You don't need to speak Japanese. There are lots of recruitment companies in Japan and many of them focus on hiring for international firms. For example, you could be helping Amazon find a bilingual marketing manager for their new product launch. The hiring managers and candidates (job seekers) likely all speak English. There are plenty of recruiters in Japan who don't speak Japanese, simply because they don't need to, as their clients and HR contacts speak English.

However, many nuances are associated with Japanese business, so if you speak zero Japanese, then this will naturally make it harder for you to relate to some of your clients and communicate with them effectively. On the other hand, if you want to use your existing

Japanese (no matter how limited), then it's an opportunity to learn proper business manners, how to negotiate, and market yourself in a different language.

A skill more important than the language used is learning about Japanese business practices. You will be faced with critical, practical questions that you didn't even know existed, such as *"where should I stand in an elevator?"* and *"what happens when I am about to hand my business card to someone and drop my business card on the floor? Should I pick up the card?"*

Yes, in Japan, there's a right and wrong way to stand in the elevator, and people do care about these seemingly minute details. Not knowing the answers to these questions could dock you points at the least or cost you business deals at worst.

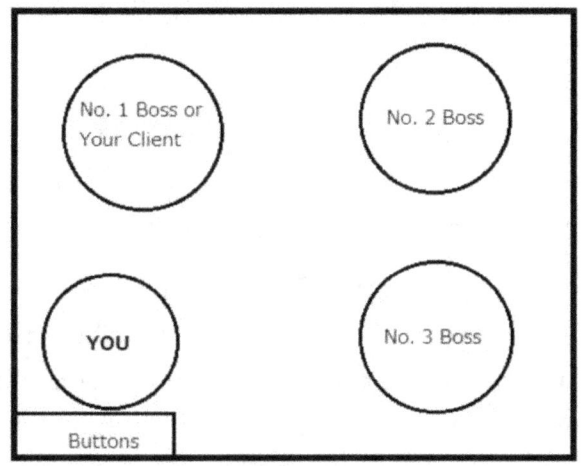

Elevator Etiquette

The other reason to join a recruitment company is simply because it's a whole lot of fun. You meet tons of people, you're out and about, and it's fast paced. Your team becomes your family. There's never a boring day as you're constantly trying to move towards the next target, build new relationships, and juggle dozens of moving pieces. In some cases, you get a generous expense account, eat at fancy restaurants, and get invited to office parties at multi-billion-dollar companies. This however shouldn't be the main reason you join the industry, of course, as there is far more hard work than there are Mojitos.

But isn't recruitment dying?

It's not dying but, rather, it's evolving. The biggest invention to disrupt the recruitment industry in the past 20 years has been the shift from the fax machine to email. I'm serious. In other words, we still have a long way to go in terms of technological advancement before the human element of recruitment is taken out of the picture and recruitment becomes totally automated. The recruitment industry is still alive and well.

There were about 3,000 registered recruitment companies in Japan in 2013. Five years later, the number had more than doubled to 7,000 registered firms. Japan's declining birth rate and economic/demographic issues have been key drivers that are contributing to the labor shortage and further fueling demand for hiring talent.

Here's the deal: Eventually, recruiters will be replaced by AI chatbots, virtual reality simulations, online platforms like a LinkedIn hybrid, or even blockchain-based. But not yet. People tend to exaggerate the pace of technological change, and we have to be realistic, considering Japan's often slow-moving bureaucratic red tape. Don't underestimate the power of talking to an actual human, especially in an job function that relies on being able to read a person and asses their alignment with a company's culture and vice versa.

That said, we're certainly seeing a new generation of recruiters emerge — less suits and more jeans. Content marketing has grown as an avenue to recruit talent and further specialization of recruiters has emerged as a trend. Focusing on niche industries rather than spreading themselves too broadly is a large part of this (i.e. being known as an expert in your field rather than having snippets of knowledge about everything). Making anonymous cold-calls no longer works, and the level of sophistication and customer service is increasing from a transactional sales approach to a more consultative approach.

Is recruitment for you?

I'm not the first to say it; recruitment is hard and not for everyone. Recruitment as an industry (internal included) has one of the highest turnover rates, meaning that many people leave after a short time, usually within 6 months to one year. It's an unfortunate statistic but one that can be avoided if you take the time to properly assess the culture of each recruitment firm you're applying to as well as understanding exactly what you're getting yourself into (this will differ from company to company), all of which I will go into shortly. This is a bit ironic because you would think recruitment companies would be good at hiring. Case in point, hiring is tough.

But why is it so tough? They say that recruitment is the business of rejection. You're always getting rejected by someone — be it a potential client, a prospective employee who doesn't want to talk to you, or someone failing an interview. Everyone fears rejection to some degree, and that's okay, we're only human. More important is your ability to bounce back from failure — in other words, your resilience. If you don't have tough skin, you'll certainly build it in the process. If you want to gauge your level of resilience and your fit for recruitment right now, a good measure is to look at other areas of your life that required tenacity. Have you ever had to work diligently and consistently at achieving something over a long period? It could be anything — running a marathon, playing piano, competitive team sports, weekly volunteer work, dance, you name it. If you've been able to spend a big chunk of time committing to mastering, or at least improving in an activity while juggling other parts of life, then you probably have at least the basic *mental* toughness to get through the guaranteed challenges you will experience being a recruiter.

On that note, an important factor to consider is the *type* of recruitment you're getting into. For example, if you're applying for a job at a large-scale agency recruitment firm like Robert Walters, their working style is going to be very different than a small boutique firm like Apex. Your personality might gel well with one firm but not the other. Indeed, you could be a great recruiter in one company but fail elsewhere, as I've seen repeatedly. We'll go through the best practices to pick the right fit for you in detail.

My first job

I joined the recruitment industry right out of college and it was one of the best decisions of my life. At the time, I had a vague idea of what recruitment was. Even after having several conversations with recruiters in Japan, it was still a black box, as I had no prior working experience, the abstract concepts and scenarios being detailed to me were hard to grasp. In the end, I chose recruitment as I saw it as an interesting opportunity to learn sales skills and build a network compared to my other options.

Your first job out of university is always going to be shrouded in some mystery — it's almost impossible to know exactly what it's going to be like to work there. This means you need to be flexible and enter the workplace with a very open mind. I was fortunate enough to have studied abroad for one year in Tokyo during university before moving back there to start work. This was an eye-opening, pivotal experience in my life, and I went through all <u>five levels</u> of Adler's culture shock—well, perhaps not the last two (recovery and reintegration phases!).

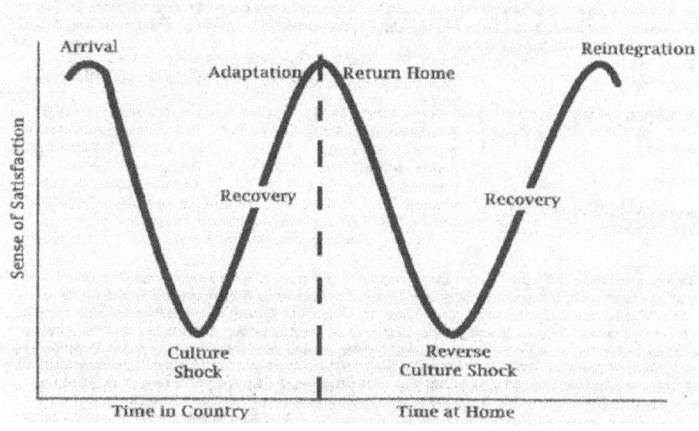

After graduation, I came back to Japan to work, so there was little culture shock to adjust to in addition to finding my way in the foreign environment of the working world. I could simply put all my efforts into the job and focus on the sales tasks in front of me without worrying about how to use chopsticks, navigating the complex train system, or getting a bank account. The recruitment job wasn't easy by any means, but my transition into work life was pretty smooth.

I observed coworkers who joined the company during the same period, many from abroad, who struggled to adjust to the culture (making friends, language) and ended up quitting after one year. When possible, try to learn the language and integrate into the culture as much as possible.

A certain level of expertise and intuition develops after doing a job for several years. Until you reach that point, though, it's hard to know where exactly to focus your time and efforts. For example, some people said "no" to working late hours. I didn't care about that. I was first man in, last man out. This paid off, as on one of my ordinarily late evenings at the office, the phone rang, I picked up, and a new account fell into my lap that proved to be profitable over the next several years.

I couldn't work late every day indefinitely, though, nor could I say yes to every colleague who wanted help with a project. When I learned the ropes, I became more conscious of my time, managed expectations, and learned what was really worth my effort.

> "Momentum begets momentum, and the best way to start is to start."
> —Gil Penchina

English Teaching to Recruitment

There are many ex-JET and English teachers who moved into recruitment. Many have excelled and made a name for themselves, doubling, tripling, and even quadrupling their salaries from 4 million to 10 million yen and above. A quick search on LinkedIn for the query "recruiter" and "JET" will bring up several results of teachers who moved from English teaching to recruitment, and from there onwards to other industries. It can serve as a starting point to give you some ideas of the sorts of career possibilities and transitions that you could take, but you don't have to limit yourself to that, of course. Since recruitment is basically a sales and marketing job, moving into a client-facing role with financial targets and goals to achieve can set you up for success in a range of industries.

Ultimately, it's a very different type of job than English teaching. Your success will come down to who you are as an individual, so it would be incorrect to assume that just because you were employed teaching English that this would determine if you could or couldn't excel at recruitment. A lot of factors need to be considered, such as the type of firm and industry, your personality, your experience level, and your boss. But the point is, that the opportunity is there. For many, the step into recruitment provides a way to learn professional communication skills, save money, pay off student loans, learn about a specific industry in depth, and even gain management experience.

For the More Experienced

There are several advantages to moving into recruitment if you've already got a few years of professional experience under your belt. Namely, it's the opportunity to be more specialized, provide better service to candidates and clients, and, ultimately, take on bigger projects. Typically, it'll be easier for you to gain trust, especially in Japan's largely seniority-based model (they'll look at your business card and consider your age).

That said, if you're joining a completely new industry or if you've been working for a company for a long time, in particular, the time it'll take you to adjust will be longer. A large part of this comes down to your own expectation setting (you never really know what it will be like to work somewhere until you've actually worked there), and simply realizing that you're not just going to "get it" immediately is important.

One study found that employees who were all-stars or "top sales people" in their previous company took, on average, 5 years to reach the same level of success when changing jobs. Transitions take time. If possible, work on some projects for the company you'd like to join beforehand, so you get a feel for the type of organizational culture and people you will be working with. The quicker you can adapt to cultural norms, workload, and so forth the faster you can build momentum.

Theories of Success

Here's a question that's well open to debate: **Are people successful because they emulate the tried and true paths of others, or are they successful in spite of them?**

In other words, if your goal is to establish yourself in Japan, earn a certain level of income, and achieve whatever 5-year goal you have, are you bound to achieve that path regardless of what I tell you in this book (due to your natural ambition/intellect)? Or, will some piece of advice or insight I share really pave the way for you?

I think the truth is likely somewhere in the middle. Some people out there have an insatiable hunger to succeed, so if you threw them into whatever situation, they'd likely figure out a way to persevere. They might heed advice from others, but it's likely they'll arrive at an approach that best suits their working style and personality. Others may very well be ambitious, but will benefit from a bit of guidance that can really jumpstart their path to achieving whatever goal they have set out for themselves. Either way, you'll be able to find some useful nuggets in this book.

Other people however, need to be pushed and dragged along to achieve their goals. They constantly seek advice and direction from others; perhaps they're great at executing tasks, but they fail at thinking outside of the box and taking action on their own. They can be effective at times, but they're not independent. Generally speaking, I've found that these sorts of people don't do very well in the recruitment industry.

I remember hiring an ex-translator as a recruiter at my previous company. She was passionate about the tech industry and wanted to get into more of a sales/marketing job. Although she had no relevant experience, I was impressed by her go-getter attitude, communication skills, and attention to detail, so I took a risk and hired her. Unfortunately, I made a mistake. We quickly discovered that she couldn't work independently and suffered from analysis paralysis. For example, she would always ask someone to double check her emails, over analyze situations, and hesitate to talk to people out of fear of not getting the "perfect" pitch. We gave her a fair chance, coached her, and she stayed on board for almost half a year, but, ultimately, she couldn't get past the daily rejection and sales aspect of the job.

Hearing this story, it's easy to compare your traits and then conclude that you are or aren't a fit for recruitment. You might have superb attention to detail and describe yourself as an analytical person, but does that mean you're probably not good at recruitment? Not at all. Some of the best recruiters I know come from engineering backgrounds. I also know a couple of great recruiters who happen to be very good at poker, too. Maybe there's a pattern there, like a penchant for risk or betting on uncertainty, but it's not fair to say that all good poker players are good recruiters. My point is that there isn't a simple formula that you can plug in and say, "Ah, yes, I am or I am not a fit." Additionally, every recruitment company has its own company culture, just like businesses in any other sector, so assessing your suitability to recruitment is not quite as black and white.

Another aspect to consider is interest in the job. You're reading this, so you have some interest in recruitment, but perhaps you're teetering on the line from English teaching or another profession. Many people mistakenly assume that you need to have a passion for something before starting it. In many cases, passion usually comes *after* action. Imagine that you're learning how to play the piano — the first few weeks there's a steep learning curve, and you basically suck. It's not that enjoyable to suck at something. Especially not for the listener. After awhile, you get better and it becomes fun to play, and maybe you get really good and it becomes your passion.

Similarly, when I first started recruitment, I had days when I thought about quitting and questioned whether it was really the right step for me. Considering that I'm an introvert, the constant phone calls to strangers were especially stressful. After I got over the initial learning curve (it took a few months), though, something clicked, and I was able to excel. I've seen people take a year to get there, and it's ultimately going to come down to you as an individual and the environment you're in.

You might be wondering: *"Doesn't recruitment have a bad reputation?"*

When people hear the word *sales* they often cringe and get flashbacks of annoying telesales people who wouldn't leave them alone. But I want you to throw this idea out the window. Twenty years ago, recruitment was full of aggressive and transactional sales people. Many of them were in it just for the money and cared little about their customers. Unfortunately, some bad apples are still out there, but, for the most part, the recruitment industry has evolved. "Sales" in recruitment has evolved from a transactional model to a more relationship, "solution-sales" model. You can't just pick up the phone anymore and get the same result. You have to be strategic, invest in learning, and build good relationships. In the long run, only those who are trustworthy, innovative, and offer real value will succeed.

> *"This is a very challenging job, but the awards are big. Also, because this job seems 'easy', since you do not require any solid education background nor experience .... actually this is what makes this job very 'difficult' as well. This job is like a race, and you are racing with other competitors, racing with your teammates, and most of all, racing with yourself."*
> **-Anthony Takashi Beasley, Executive Recruiter at PAL K.K.**

CHAPTER 1
THE RECRUITMENT MODEL EXPLAINED

Why do recruitment agencies exist?

Recruitment seeks to solve a fundamental problem — how do you hire and retain the best people? Let's say that Apple wants to enter the Chinese market and set up a branch tomorrow. They need to find a Country Head to start up the office. If it takes Apple 6 months to find that person, what is the opportunity cost of waiting? Well, the Country Head also has to hire a sales team, partner with distributors, and get through legal hurdles. In reality, the delay could mean that it could take them a year before they start selling their iPhones.

If Apple would have found that hire in 4 months, or 1 month, instead of 6, they could have started selling millions of iPhones, grossing hundreds of millions of dollars far sooner. For every second they don't have the person to do this job, they're losing out on a *lot* of money. This is the value you can add as recruiter, and this is exactly why companies are willing to pay so much money to recruitment agencies to find the right people. That's the client side, and *client* here (Apple in this example) refers to the company that is paying a recruitment company to source talent for them.

On the other side of the equation, we have candidates. *Candidate* is just a synonym for job seeker. Why would someone looking for a job use a recruiter rather than just applying for the job directly? That's simple. First of all, recruiters have specialized knowledge about the company, the job, and the interview process that you couldn't get access to otherwise. They can manage the interview process as well as both your expectations and the client's. They know what skills are required to actually landt the job, and often can put you directly in touch with the decision makers rather than you just dealing with HR who, in some cases, do not necessarily have a broad grasp of what the role entails nor the authority to make final hiring calls.

Recruiters have insight into current market trends - they can tell you whether or not a company has a good reputation, divulging information about what it's really like to work there, not just what's written online or presented in carefully crafted company profiles and introductory meetings. A great recruiter can give you objective advice about whether the role you are eyeing is actually a good career move based on your long term goals. Good recruiters can help you negotiate your salary and favorable job terms. They can be the difference between getting your dream job because of a direct recommendation from someone the company trusts, versus submitting your application along with hundreds of others through the company job page and never getting a response from HR.

"Recruitment seeks to solve a fundamental problem — how do you hire and retain the best people?"

How does recruitment work?

As an agency recruiter, a company (client) will pay you a fee for successfully hiring a candidate (the person looking for a job). You get paid by clients, *not* the candidates. A very important point to remember.

The fee is calculated based on a percentage of the candidate's agreed upon yearly salary. For example, if Amazon hires an engineer at an annual salary of 8,000,000 yen, then the recruitment company will receive 35% of the package (8 million multiplied by .35 = 2,800,000 yen) as a one-off fee. Now, that fee doesn't go into your bank account, but it is added to your overall "target" for the quarter. Your actual salary and commission % earned will depend on the bonus and incentive system that your company has set up.

Two types of recruiters:

1. *Internal recruiters*, also known as "corporate" recruiters, work directly for the employer's organization and usually collect a paycheck

(salary) from the business who has the job's vacancies. Their office will typically be on the employer's premises, and their email and phone will typically be part of the employer's email and phone system.
2. *External recruiters,* also known as agency recruiters, do not receive a paycheck from the employer (client) looking to hire staff. They work for an external party, a recruiting firm or agency, that issues their paychecks. Some, of course, work for themselves.

I am biased towards agency recruitment, as that's where my speciality was, so this guide will be largely from that perspective; however, many of the principles are applicable across the entire industry.

Here are the different recruitment **models and definitions** to familiarize yourself with:

1. *Contingency recruitment* means that, as a recruiter, you'll get paid *after* the client hires your candidates. You get no upfront fee, but only get paid upon completion of the search (finding the candidate) and, usually, a couple of weeks after the candidate's first day of work.
2. *Retained search or retainers* means that the client is paying you an initial, upfront fee to help them hire someone. Usually, the fee is nonrefundable. This means they have a higher expectation of you finding a highly qualified candidate. You'll

have to map out the market, provide weekly reports, and provide a tailored, prioritized service as they're paying you a large sum up front.
3. ***Executive Recruitment*** refers to hiring senior and C-level employees: Directors, VPs, and CEOs. Usually, executive recruitment firms operate on a retained search model.
4. ***Haken recruitment or staffing*** refers to dispatch and temporary staff recruitment. The client needs someone to work on a temporary basis. The recruitment temp agency hires temporary workers from a pool on a regular basis and sends them on assignment to work at its client companies.
5. ***Contract recruitment*** is non permanent recruitment, usually shorter 3 month-1 year assignments. Contract employment has some stigma in Japan; however, many contract workers are highly skilled, paid very well, and often convert into permanent employees.
6. ***Permanent recruitment*** means an employee will be hired on a full-time contract.
7. ***Search, recruitment, staffing, or headhunting.*** These words are all synonyms and are used interchangeably.
8. ***Sourcing*** simply refers to finding the candidates who have suitable skills for a job. A sourcing associate/ manager is not an end-to-end recruiter.

Rather, a sourcer creates interest and drives talent to the organization. This means doing research: pouring over organisational charts, job descriptions, and social media profiles, and hitting search engines and competitors' Web pages.
9. *End-to-end recruitment* refers to the full process of finding both candidates and clients to work with, and managing the whole process right from taking a full brief on the requirements of the vacancy all the way to placing suitable candidates in those roles. Often, a recruitment company will hire a newcomer as a sourcing manager for a few months and then promote them to an end-to-end recruiter.

The Flow of the Recruitment Process

Unless you've worked in recruitment before or worked for a company interfacing with HR, the recruitment process is likely opaque. I remember on my first day as a recruiter, I didn't even know who was paying us or how we were making money, let alone what I would actually be doing on the job.

Here's the basic flow of what the recruitment process looks like, and what a recruiter does from start (finding clients/candidates) to finish (getting job offers for candidates). There are about a million steps in between, but this is the bare bones that will be sufficient for interview purposes.

There are essentially two areas that all of your activities will be split into, and it will be helpful to think about it from both the candidate perspective (job seeker) and from the client side (company).

The candidate side includes but is not limited to the following activities:

- Scouting for new potential candidates on Linkedin and other job boards
- Meeting new candidates to discuss potential job opportunities and assess their suitability to the vacancies at hand

- Remeeting previous candidates to discuss job opportunities
- Preparing candidates for interviews
- Scheduling interviews for candidates
- Negotiating offers and compensation on behalf of candidates

The client side includes but is not limited to the following activities:

- Finding new clients (business development calls, going to marketing events)
- Attending new client meetings
- Negotiating contracts and fees with clients
- Attending catch up meetings with existing clients ("account management")
- Updating clients on the status of a search
- Scheduling interviews on behalf of candidates with the client company

Also, you'll have your own internal meetings to deal with like team meetings or catch ups with your boss. Technically, then, you have three main groups of activities to manage: the candidate, client, and internal.

A Day in the Life of a Recruiter

What is the job actually like and what do recruiters do? No day is the same in recruitment. That's the fun part; you have a lot of autonomy to make your own schedule. It's a lot like running your own company. It also makes it challenging because *you and only you* are responsible for your success.

The goal is to find the best hires for your clients, so most of your time is spent with that goal in mind. That entails everything from finding the candidates, helping them with interview preparation, negotiating contracts, exchanging feedback with clients, and influencing the hiring process. You manage several clients, who have several job openings, and you could be helping anywhere from 10-20 people find jobs at any given time. You will spend a significant amount of time understanding the market, meeting candidates, meeting clients, interviewing, screening, negotiating, and building relationships.

Typically a recruiter's year is split up into four 3-month quarters, where revenue and targets are all tallied up over those 3-month periods. I've found that the first month is usually the most intense and busiest as you spend time building up a foundation of candidates for that quarter. The second month is less busy and "tapers off" as you spend more time scheduling interviews and preparing candidates, which you found during the first month, and the third month of the quarter is spent closing those deals and gets busy again. That's just a general observation, though, and it can differ across industries, seasons, and other circumstances.

Here's an example of what your day might look like:

6:00 am : You wake up, consume copious amounts of coffee, do 50 pushups, maybe some yoga, and get ready for a great day. You listen to Tony Robbins audio books and TED Talks on the way to work as you're always pushing to educate yourself. You're excited.

8:00 am : You arrive at the office 30 minutes early to get a head start; your blood is rushing from the caffeine and positive energy. You quickly check your emails to make sure you don't have any urgent actions to take. You write a crafty email for a contract negotiation with a company that you're trying to bring on as a client. You look at your calendar and plan your day for 5 minutes, determining the most important actions to take. You also make a quick business-development (BD) call into a company you've been trying to bring on as a client because you know that CEOs and directors are usually in the office early and you'll have a higher likelihood of catching them.

8:30 am : You have a standing team meeting to discuss the most "active" candidates in the job market and what kind of opportunities they might be interested in. Using the customer-relationship-management (CRM) system (the interface looks a lot like Facebook), you take note of which teammate will be "pitching" (introducing a new job opportunity) to whom during the morning. You decide if you have any specific jobs to pitch to them.

You prepare a list of 30 candidates that you intend on calling this morning to pitch.

9:00 am - 11:00 am : Game time! You pick up the phone and start *smiling and dialing*. You don't sit when you call; you stand, because you know that you can breathe easier, move more freely, and sound more confident standing up. Most people don't pick up the phone, so you leave voicemails and emails. One person answers the phone and asks you to add them on Line messenger (Japan's most popular messaging service), as they're at work in their office and can't talk on the phone. A couple of people reject you on the spot, and your ego takes a small blow. The feeling only lasts for one second before your pick up the phone again and call the next person. One person, Tanaka-san, answers your call, and you end up speaking with him for 30 minutes about the job opportunity at Amazon. You have a great conversation. He seems very interested, and agrees to send his resume to you so that you can forward his application to Amazon.

11:00 am : You receive an sudden phone call from one of your candidates who is supposed to interview today. He says he's running 15 minutes late, and sounds panicked. You calm him down on the phone, reassure him, and then call the client to inform them that the interviewee is running slightly late.

11:30 am - noon : You spend 30 minutes crafting a new job description for the position at Amazon to make it more appealing to candidates. Your boss sends you a message asking to help with time-management training for new starters next week. It sounds like fun and you're more than happy to do so, even though your time-management skills aren't exactly great.

Noon-1:30 pm : At the Grand Hyatt, you have lunch with a candidate who recently started the job that you placed (introduced) her into. She seems very happy as she was able to double her salary and is fitting right into the company culture. You feel great that you were able to make a positive impact on someone's life. The purpose of this lunch was to celebrate, maintain a long-term relationship, and make sure that things are going well with the new job. At the end of the lunch, she refers you to a friend of hers who works at Google and is looking for a job.

2:00 pm - 3:00 pm : You've strategically planned your next meeting down the street from the Grand Hyatt, where you're meeting Toshimoto-san to help him prepare for his job interview next week. You come prepared to do interview role plays with him, and dispel any questions and concerns he has before the interview.

3:00 pm - 3:30 pm: You whip out your phone and go straight onto Google.com. You then cram as much information into your mind about Nike, a new client that you're about to meet with in 30 minutes time. You should have prepared earlier, but the week has been crazy busy — it's always a race against time. So you look up everything about Nike online, their products, financials, and strategy. *(If you were good at cramming in school, you might do well here!)*

3:30 – 5:00 pm : This is your first client meeting with a new company — Nike. You're meeting with the Marketing Director and come to the meeting prepared with a dozen questions and resumes. Despite your late cramming to prepare for the meeting, they agree to a contract with a 35% fee. Score - you share a status update about this victory with the team on *Slack* messenger.

5:00-6:30 pm : You find a quiet cafe and sit down to finish administrative and paperwork. You input information about the meetings you had today on your companies CRM system, check your schedule for tomorrow, and take a couple of phone calls. You also send 5 candidates' resumes to companies.

6:30 pm - 8:00 pm: There's a casual networking event tonight at a bar in Ebisu where you think you can meet potential candidates. You have a couple of glasses of wine, dinner, and exchange business cards with people. You learn about a new advertising-technology company from Israel that is planning to enter the Japanese market, so you make a note on your phone to do some research on it tomorrow and possibly reach out to stakeholders.

8:30 pm: You finally get home — whew, what a day! You feel accomplished. You chug a glass of water and check your emails one more time to make sure there is no urgent mail. Today was a good day and you're excited about what tomorrow will bring. You shower, read a few pages from a business book about *Rakuten* written by the founder Hiroshi Mikitani-san, and fall asleep.

> What does a good day look like?
> *"A combination of productive "desk work" and getting key things done, plus an external meeting and relationship building."*
> -**Romen Barua, Tokyo Supercars CEO / Konnex COO**

CHAPTER 2
THE JAPANESE MARKET

The Japanese market has some of the highest recruitment fees in the world, hovering around 35%. There are some companies who pay 40%, 50% and even 100% fees! Compare this to the rest of the world (U.S. average fee is 20%, UK 10-15%); these low numbers are ridiculous.

Here are the reasons why fees in Japan are so high:

1) Japanese people do not frequently change their jobs, so it's simply harder to get people interested in switching their jobs. This is partly cultural, since people are more risk-averse and see the interview process as very "formal," but it stems largely from the archaic lifetime employment system that emerged post-WWII.

2) Supply and Demand. The price of goods and services (like buying a house or car) is determined by the market, similarly, the low supply of candidates and high demand of job vacancies tilts the market to make

each individual more valuable in the eyes of the employer. Japan has a labor shortage. There are 2.4 job openings for every applicant. This is the opposite of an unemployment problem that many other countries face.

3) The number of English speakers is strikingly low, so the pool of bilingual, or multilingual, candidates is very low, which creates more competition for skilled candidates. In particular, foreign firms like Amazon have a much harder time hiring than Japanese firms who don't need bilingual talent, although the demand for labor is tight across virtually all industries in Japan.

4) It's hard to fire people. Japanese labor laws are very strict and side with the employee, so if you're fired, it's not only a frustrating, long process that requires lots of documentation, but it's also bad for the company's reputation and easy for the employee to sue. One way companies avoid this is by hiring people on a temporary one-year contract, and it's starting to become a more popular option (Google does this often).

5) Big recruitment firms like "Recruit" (they own Indeed) set the market rates for fees, and keep them elevated, as they obviously have a good incentive to keep fees high.

> *"Everyone talks about the economy and Abenomics. In Japan, the temporary recruitment market in fiscal 2014 grew 105%. The permanent market grew 118%. Companies are so short on good staff. It doesn't affect us on a day-to-day basis."*
> —Lanis Yarzab, Managing Director of Spring Japan

Lifetime Employment and a Bit of Cultural Context

After WWII, Japanese companies developed the lifetime employment system, which still exists to some degree today. Every year, companies round up students right out of school and push them through a soul-killing "job hunting" (shukatsu) process, at the end of which they often accept jobs at large, stable companies and are then employed there for life. The employee gets a nice stable job, subsidized housing, and modest salary increases over time. In return, the employer gets a loyal employee for decades.

The bonus system in Japan is usually annual or biannual, and has traditionally not been based on individual performance, but on company performance. Company profits = everyone gets a bonus. No company profits = no one gets a bonus. In other words, it's not really merit based, although this has certainly started to change, in particular, among the tech-related companies.

Leaving your job or changing your job frequently was

simply less common in Japan up until the past few years (in particular the 2008 financial crisis shook things up and Japanese realized their jobs weren't safe, as did many people in the world). Large Japanese companies put employees on a job function conveyor belt, requiring them to change their roles every couple of years (from HR, to sales, to marketing, operations, and so forth). This resulted in employees who never really develop a high level of proficiency in one area, becoming generalists rather than specialists, further exacerbating the labor shortage, as finding specific skill sets is far trickier.

The mentality of "company comes first" rather than "the individual comes first" is deeply ingrained in the psyches of middle-aged men who are running Japanese companies. That won't disappear overnight. Forfeiting your individual rights (work *is* family) has led to all sorts of issues, namely a sort of self-flagellation in the name of the intangible thing known as "company," and a ton of overworked people. Despite what the labor statistics say, most overtime still goes unreported.

In his widely popular, witty and controversial book, *Straightjacket Society*, Dr. Masao Miyamoto wrote extensively about the inefficiencies and mindless bureaucracy back in the 80s and 90s. He describes a "voluntary" company trip that he took to a hot spring (onsen); the weekend trip was work-related and counted as "unpaid overtime." It consisted of getting madly drunk, watching porn in the hotel room, and singing karaoke songs together (mind you, these are middle-aged bureaucrats spending tax-money and responsible for running the country).

Speaking to several of his colleagues, Miyamoto realized that, like him, most of them didn't *actually* want to be there. They would have rather spent the weekend with their families, but social-pressure and the need to appease bosses wouldn't allow it. This highly group-oriented system worked for Japan during a time of economic catch-up postwar, but from even before Miyamoto's time, it started to lose its edge.

The system further disintegrated after the 2009 financial crisis when more and more people were laid off, crushing the long-held belief that a company will have your back for life. Miyamoto was highly critical of the group-think mentality, but he didn't tout Western individualism to be the silver-bullet. Like most things in life, he believed that there was likely a middle path; teamwork and respect for the elders espoused by Japanese, mixed in with a sense of individuality and freedom of expression from the West.

The labor laws in Japan are notoriously strict; even amidst lay-offs, the law is on the side of *employee*, which means it's very difficult to fire people. The expression "to get fired" translates to "クビになる," which literally means to get *necked*. This has direct origins from the 17th century Edo Period practice of beheading criminals or samurai who betrayed the clan. The structural, legal and cultural barriers around firing makes labor movement slow and less liquid. Everybody loses.

One solution Japanese companies have adopted is to hire more contract workers on a yearly basis (rather than permanent employees), thus giving both sides more flexibility to go their separate ways after this period. Google Japan, for example, hires almost all of its employees on a contract basis. This approach has worked to an extent — it's a positive, incremental push in the right direction. Prime Minister Abe's goal to increase female participation in the work force seems to be making strides. Individually this is not enough to address Japan's labor shortage or rewind Japan's demographic time bomb, but it's addressing one piece of the puzzle.

Yoshie Komuro's work is another great step. Any meaningful change in Japan is based on precedent, and once we have enough leaders like her, enough large and reputable companies willing to change, then I could see it snowball into positive change (rather, the companies that aren't jumping on board to the new system will feel socially pressured to do so). A couple of years ago Komuro-san worked with Mie Prefecture to start a "Work Life Balance Promotion Project" that involved a range of seminars and reforms across 13 local companies in the prefecture.

The campaign's aim was largely to spread awareness of work-life balance issues and slowly plant seeds in the minds of stubborn senior management. Part of the campaign involved making employees aware that they could take consecutive days off for longer holidays (Wed-Sunday), which they tend to hesitate to do for fear of being reprimanded. They also provided training on hand-over procedures when a colleague went on holiday and encouraged companies to create better organizational processes to foster this.

This may seem so blatantly obvious to a Westerner working for a tech company in the U.S. that some may feel that there's no hope for Japan's arcane labor policies — but remember, big change is incremental. Moreover, the results were promising.

> "the result was a 15% increase in labor productivity (gross profit divided by the number of employees) from the previous year.[...] In one case, employees' use of paid vacation days tripled. Elsewhere, the number of marriages doubled, and births rose 2.5-fold. The birthrate in Mie Prefecture as a whole is on the rise as well. When the husband's work-life balance improves, the wife feels more confident about having that second child."

Actually, that's pretty impressive. Politicians in Japan are banging their heads trying to figure out how to increase marriage rates (which is essentially tied to birth rates in Japan), spur innovation, and boost economic productivity. Maybe it's as simple as just taking more days off work and going home earlier? Well, it's certainly part of it. Surely when there are enough use-cases and precedent, then the seemingly obvious (we're not productive working 15 hour days) will "click" with the politicians. On the other hand, I wonder what will happen first—meaningful change in Japanese labor markets, AI replacing human jobs, and/or Chinese people replacing the Japanese population in the next few decades? Only time will tell.

What does this all mean for recruitment?

This all means that it continues to be difficult to pull people from their companies. I mean, why would you leave your cushy, stable job where you know that you'll get promoted when you get older? Granted, things are changing and the Japanese market is a lot more *"liquid"* now. Liquidity just means there's more movement of people from company to company, especially in the technology sector. San Francisco has a very liquid market, as people change jobs frequently.

However, services like LinkedIn are still relatively unpopular in Japan (only about 1 million users). The job search process in Japan is seen as very formal, and it takes, on average, several weeks to complete an interview and then another 4-6 weeks before candidates join. Compare this to the U.S. where you can interview, have an offer within a week and start work 2 weeks later.

The challenge in hiring further indicates that companies are really struggling to innovate in Japan because they don't have the people to do so. It means that, as a recruiter, if you specialize and know all of the best candidates in your specific industry, then you have a huge advantage. It also means you need to spend time building deeper relationships with candidates (sometimes hand-holding them through the interview process), since they're more hesitant to change jobs than their Western counterparts.

The salaries for sales, marketing, and engineering jobs within foreign tech companies in Japan are continuing to rise because of a labor shortage (low supply of bilingual, skilled talent and high demand). Compared to 5 years ago, companies like Amazon, Google, and Expedia are more willing to pay top dollar in Japan.

In order for Japan to compete in a global market, there will have to be labor reforms and structural changes. The government has helped in some ways by encouraging female workers to get back into the workforce after having kids — a largely untapped labor force. But it's just a start. I believe many of the problems are also largely cultural (work culture, stagnant HR departments) and will require a combined effort of both government and the private sector. This will either happen with time, as a new, more progressive generation of CEOs and executives grow their companies in Japan and replace the archaic-minded incumbents, setting a new example for people and companies to follow. Or perhaps this may come about through the aggressive expansion of foreign businesses into Japan that are able to equally set a new standard, but I suspect this approach would take longer.

For now, the labor market remains very tight, hiring is tough, and the value of finding great talent continues to rise.

The big recruitment players in Japan:

Executive Recruitment

- Korn Ferry
- Heidrick and Struggles
- Egon Zehnder
- Spencer Stuart

Large Contingency Recruitment Firms

- Recruit
- Intelligence
- Robert Walters
- Hays
- RGF
- Michael Page
- Enworld

Small/Midsize Recruitment Firms

- Morgan McKinley
- Wahl & Case
- Optia Partners

- CDS
- Robert Half
- East West Consulting

Staffing/Haken

- Randstad
- Manpower
- Recruit
- Pasona
- Robert Walters

Online Recruitment Platforms

- LinkedIn
- Daijob
- Gaijinpot
- Wantedly
- Careercross

Other places to apply directly for recruitment jobs

- <u>Wantedly</u> - This is a Japanese site that takes a more "casual" approach to job hunting. You can message companies directly and request a call or meeting in their office to hang out with the team for a few hours. It's not really in an interview style and quite easy to get your foot in the door. If the chemistry is there, then the next step would be formal interviews.
  https://jp.wantedly.com/

- Justa - They are geared mostly towards foreign/Japanese startup companies based in Tokyo. Seventy percent of the jobs are more tech/dev related but there are some sales/marketing roles too.
  https://justa.io/

- GaijinPot - They have a lot of jobs for non-Japanese speakers that generally fall into three categories: recruitment, teaching, or translation.
  https://gaijinpot.com/

- Bizreach - This one is harder to navigate because it's all in Japanese, but just translate the page using google translate and sign up. Apart from LinkedIn Japan, it's one of the top sites for finding mid level jobs and upwards across various industries.
  https://www.bizreach.jp/

- Techinasia - A tech focused blogging and media site that lists jobs across Asia, with a specific section for Japan and a large networking event they hold each year.
  https://www.techinasia.com/

- WorkshiftSolutions - This is a freelance site that has the most registered non-Japanese people in Japan. It's a good place to test the waters and pick up some projects that could potentially turn into longer term/permanent jobs.
  https://workshift-sol.com/

You'll find that many of the recruitment companies listed above have recruitment jobs listed on LinkedIn, so you can start with an application directly through their portal. The other option is to directly submit your application through their websites. I would do both, considering HR can get quite busy and you never know which site they'll check. We'll get more into how to apply shortly, but it's also important to keep in mind the different synonyms for *recruiter*, which will be helpful when you're looking at job titles.

The following words all mean recruiter:

- Recruiter
- Headhunter
- Associate Consultant
- Consultant
- Sourcer
- Recruitment Agent
- Recruitment specialist
- Search
- Executive search specialist
- Career consultant
- Talent sourcing specialist

CHAPTER 3:

HOW TO SELECT THE RIGHT COMPANY

Which recruitment company and style is right for you?

This is a great question and one that will ultimately determine your success in the company. The type of recruiter you become will be based on:

1. Your own ethics and values and
2. The environment you're in, which creates your incentives.

Number 1 is a matter of personal self-assessment, and number 2 is a matter of culture fit with the company. If you're starting out in recruitment, especially if this is your first job, I suggest starting out in agency recruitment, as there are more options and the barrier to entry is lower. Also, especially in mid/larger sized firms, you'll get very good training. Many people will start out in a large firm, and then, after a year, will jump to a smaller firm where they can be more specialized. Remember, recruitment years are like dog years.

To join an executive search firm or get appointed into an internal recruitment role usually requires some industry knowledge or an existing network — if you have that, great. Once you're in the industry, it's much easier to go internal or join a more specialized firm.

Everyone will have a different style and values, so determine what's right for you. Then use this as a lens to assess different recruitment companies during the interview process. I would always give companies the benefit of the doubt when interviewing, so if you find one aspect of the job you don't like through the interview, don't cancel the rest of your interviews. It's almost always worth seeing out the interview process to the end to get a fuller picture of the company as well as interview practice.

Here's a checklist of areas that you should assess:

Culture: What are the values of the company? What kind of people do they have working there now? Do people work as a team, or is it individual-based? Who is the CEO, and what are their goals for the company? How quick is the decision making process? Is the company fast-growing or is it closer to a "lifestyle" business? Is it a Japanese recruitment firm or foreign firm?

KPI's: Key Performance Indicators. These are the metrics that the company/manager will use to assess your performance. You will live and breathe these, so it's important that you're crystal clear on these. If you have to make 50 calls per day, is that the sort of environment you want to be in? Find out what these are and what the expectations are for consultants. KPIs could include the number of resumes you send per week, the number of candidates you meet face-to-face, the number of job interviews you secure for your applicants per week, and the number of clients you've met.

Company Size: Generally larger recruitment companies have better training programs, smaller ones don't, although there are exceptions. I would ask the recruitment company exactly what their program looks like and even request a schedule to see how in depth it looks. If they say they don't have one and it's more "on the job (OTJ) training," I wouldn't recommend it, unless you already know how the recruitment industry works and are comfortable stepping into that sort of environment. On the other hand, smaller companies tend to be more flexible and bigger ones more rigid with their expectations and requirements, but then there's a trade off of stability of the company. What's the right fit for you?

Recruiter Tom Wish from Hunted breaks it down very well, so I've listed a Japan-specific version of his blog post here:

Advantages of of working for a larger recruitment firm
The buzz of a big sales floor. Inspires competitiveness and the thrill of doing a deal surrounded by multiple teams
If you're top biller: the bigger the company the bigger the achievement
Infrastructure: The almighty database isn't the advantage it used to be over your competition, but it's still an advantage. Especially when starting in a new market. The more established the company, the larger the pool for you to cast your net
The training and development is likely to be more advanced, more refined and have benefitted from more financial investment
There will almost certainly be larger budgets for marketing activities and you probably even [have] a separate marketing team
A global (and usually positive, [but not always]) reputation even before you introduce yourself on the phone which can really help with business development
Potential for a more diverse career e.g. Non-billing manager, Managed Services, RPO, Training and

development [again, this of course depends]
The financial stability of the company is always a bonus, and may mean you get paid commission in the period when offer is accepted/invoiced rather than waiting until it has been paid
Potentially bigger incentives: whether that's better holiday destinations or a just a bigger budget for team drinks on a Friday
A wider benefits package
You won't know everyone in the company (hello Christmas party!)
Share options (if possible) may offer reward sooner, if the company is on track to an event (IPO/sale)

Advantages of working for a smaller recruitment firm
Greater exposure to Founders and Directors as mentors and to learn from. Not to mention there being fewer layers of management between you and the decision makers. [When I was in recruitment, I would have lunch with the CEO often; furthermore, decision making was faster because I could pitch him ideas directly]

A much lower business cost can often often mean a more attractive reward or commission structure
You can help define the working environment and take an active part in its direction
There's probably a greater chance to be entrepreneurial and build something from scratch. Nothing gives you more pride than building your own business
A potential for equity and ownership at an earlier stage of the business growth
A heightened sense of team spirit (and potentially less star candidates hidden in someone's top drawer)
Typically more autonomy and flexibility
More opportunity to take a lead in diversification. Such as opening a new office in a new location
The incentives may be more creative and have you in mind and not subject to so many approvals
More agile and faster to adapt. Whether that's adopting new CRM or moving into a different market specialism
You're more likely to know everyone at the company
Your own day job may be more varied. If there's no

> marketing function, guess what you can add to your CV?

> It's easier to find an ideal fit of company, given the vast choice of smaller companies: You can consider culture, rewards, leadership, offices, sector, team, direction of company, worldwide location etc. (most recruitment firms in Japan have 30 employees and under)

Industry: Are you passionate about the pharmaceutical industry? Finance? E-commerce? IT? Startups? Fashion? How much Japanese would you need to use? Is it easy to switch industries and teams within the recruitment company once joined? Often, it's not, especially if it's a smaller company. You can narrow down your search of recruitment agencies based on the industries they cover, although this information isn't always accessible online and the specific openings are going to often depend on timing.

Function. Similar to industry, the function you focus on is going to heavily influence the sort of network you build as well as the types of people you'll talk to on a daily basis. This can also be influenced by your own personality. For example, I was working in mostly sales/marketing recruitment, so a majority of the people I met were easy going and good communicators. This was a great fit for my personality because I am interested in marketing and have done some sales work through part time jobs. However, if you're working with engineers or operations/finance, for example, this might (but not always) require you to adopt a different approach to everything from how you communicate to how you search for people.

The Team: Who are the people you'll be working with every day? If you were stuck on a plane with these people for 12 hours, would you gouge your eyes out? You can do some digging on LinkedIn to see who works at the company and their backgrounds. I recommend spending as much time as you can with the team and people in the company before making a decision to join, as you'll often learn more about the business from informal meetings than you will in a stuffy interview room.

Your Boss: Your direct manager will make or break your success in recruitment. Don't underestimate this. If they're supportive and provide hands-on training, you can shine. If not, then you'll become another statistic. Most people leave their jobs because they're unhappy with their bosses. You want to ask them what their management style is, their best and worst hire, what they think makes someone successful on the job, and how their management style has evolved. Also, make sure to spend, at minimum, 2-3 hours with them to get to know them.

Compensation package/salary: What is the base and

bonus structure? How is the bonus determined? Is it a quarterly bonus, biannual, yearly bonus? What is the expectation in the first 3 months? What is the worst case and best case salary scenarios for a first-year hire in the company? Is it a team-based bonus pool, a draw-system, or 100% commission? If you're starting out, I suggest aiming for a company that has a relatively generous base salary. If you are more confident in your existing network/abilities, then you can target a higher bonus/commission structure (great risk, higher reward).

If a recruitment company is in an industry you're not interested in and is a small firm, then perhaps it's completely out of the question for you, and, thus, you're not going to apply. You'll realize that you won't be able to assess *most* of these criteria until you actually meet the company, but you should start gathering information beforehand.

No company is going to have a perfect set of criteria. You might have a great culture and a great boss, but the pay might be rather low. Where will you make a trade off? What's more important to you? This will, of course, vary from person to person, it's important to keep in mind that the above are just guidelines to help you assess a company before, during, and after interviews.

Many people also use Glassdoor to get information about the company. This is okay as one reference point, but it's not the be all and end all. Company cultures do change, so reviews can be outdated, and Glassdoor shouldn't be the reason you do or don't apply. Food for thought: Usually, the people who add reviews on Glassdoor are those who have something to complain about. And, usually, people who spend their time complaining are the least successful in life.

Once you've chosen a few companies you'd like to apply to, you're almost ready to submit a resume.

CHAPTER 4

HOW TO LAND THE INTERVIEW

What to include in your Resume (CV) and Cover Letter

- Keep your resume simple, one page is fine, although there's no rule to keep to only one. Don't bother with fancy fonts or colors. Here's a link to a good, clean resume template that you can use.
- Put your top three attributes that you can bring to the job at the very top. This is key, as the very top of the resume is where you can capture the attention of the person reading it. You have 0.2 seconds to do so.
- What transferable skills can you bring if you have no job experience? Some of the most important ones for recruitment are persistence/commitment to one task (sport, hobby), customer-facing or people-facing experience, and working under

deadlines/pressure. Don't be afraid to include seemingly unrelated industry experience.
- In the case of Japan, having some knowledge of the language and culture is a huge plus, so it's crucial to include this as well.
- Think about this: where in your life have you shown persistence and tenacity (they are two slightly different traits). Six years in tennis club? What about teamwork? Boy scouts? What about customer service? Part-time job at McDonalds? Nothing? What about 1 year studying Japanese, and the commitment you made? All these things count.

Here's the difference between persistence and tenacity. Recruiters value tenacity, the ability to <u>persist while continuously improving</u> (this is not a factory plant where you're doing the same thing day in and day out, after all). Tenacity is also the quality of being able to persist in the face of failure or setbacks, being able to continue and move forward without letting failures derail your focus on achieving your goal. Review your past jobs and extracurricular activities, projects, and events you've been involved in to come up with examples of how you've been tenacious in the past.

PERSISTENCE
VERSUS
TENACITY

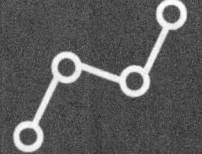

The persistent writer continues to apply the same methods, even if flawed

The tenacious writer analyses results and implements positive changes

Mr Persistence develops a pitch template for prospecting

Mrs Tenacious also develops a pitch template for prospecting

He receives a response rate of 10%, most are rejections

She receives a response rate of 10%, most are rejections

Mr Persistent recycles his template and tries again

Mrs Tenacious researches better pitches, seeks expert advice, and analyses every approach before improving her template and trying again

He receives a response rate of 10%, most are rejections

She receives a 15% response rate, most of which express interest

Sending your application

I have a friend who sent his application to 100 companies and did not get a response from any of them. Zero. Zilch. Nada. After digging a bit deeper, I found that he was sending the exact same resume to all the companies, applied directly to their websites, and never followed up with any of them. He was doing it totally wrong. Tailoring your approach and focusing on **quality** will get you better results than spamming people with your resume.

I'm confident that you can get feedback from any company you apply to if you approach it properly. No more waiting around for companies to call you. Yes, really.

Here's what you should do, step by step:

- Create a one-page cover letter and customize it for the company and the role that you're applying to.
- Visit the company's website and submit your resume along with your cover letter.
- Wait 24 hours…no response…

This is where most people give up. But not you. You're tenacious. There's a huge difference between taking a *passive approach* to something versus an *active approach*. Waiting around will never get you anywhere and you must take matters into your own hands. So, next, get on Google and look up the phone number of the company. Nobody makes phone calls anymore, but as Mr. T would say, "I pity the fool." In other words, people will pick up the phone when you call. Recruiters love it, so by simply picking up the phone and calling in, you set yourself up for getting an interview. Moreover, companies in Japan still use landlines, so it's not as uncommon as perhaps the U.S. or Europe.

When you call them, ask for their HR person, and say the following:

> *"Hi, my name is John and I've recently applied through your website for a position as a recruitment consultant. I haven't heard back yet so wanted to check on the status of my application."*

You'll either be told that they're still reviewing your resume, or that they'll get back to you.

> *"Great, roughly when should I expect a response?"*

If you still don't hear back from the company within the next 48 hours, don't wait around.

Go on LinkedIn and create an account if you haven't done so already. Take some time to make it look nice, fill in everything. LinkedIn is your best friend. Go to the search bar and type in the name of the company you're applying to, followed by "senior manager," "director," or "managing director." You are going to message someone at the company directly.

So for example your query would look like this:

> *"XX Recruitment Company" AND "director"*

A list of results will pop up listing people who currently work at that company with titles containing the word director. Select the top three and send them a request to "connect." Wait for them to accept your connection, and then send them a message. Alternatively, you can download the Hunter Chrome extension to find their emails faster.

> *"Dear Bob, my name is John and I'm currently an English teacher at XX...I'm very interested in developing a career in recruitment, and believe I have what it takes. I'd be excited to have an opportunity to talk to you and your company about potential job openings. My email is X and you can reach my cell at xxx-xxx-xxx."*

Great, now you've sent your application online, called into their company, and messaged someone high up in the organization. That's 99% more than most people do. Repeat this process and you *will* get a response (unless everyone in the company mysteriously disappears).

> "Two things I would recommend when trying to get into recruiting firms are: Practice interviewing at firms you aren't that interested in and use LinkedIn to get your foot in the door. Again, your personality and attitude will be a big deciding factor on whether or not you're going to be hired so get as comfortable with the interviews as you possibly can. Saying all the right things could easily

make up for a crappy resume. After you practice at the firms that you aren't interested, make a list of the firms you really want to get in. Rank them from neutral to most positive and interview at the most positive ones last. Since almost any recruiter will be on LinkedIn and they are typically more than happy to connect with most people, LinkedIn could really help you get your foot in the door and put you a step ahead of just applying through their hiring website. Send a connection request to recruiters with a short message explaining you are looking for work in Japan and you are hoping for some introductions.

-Luke Palfrey, Recruiter at Enworld

CHAPTER 5

THE INTERVIEW PROCESS

A typical interview at a recruitment firm will look something like this. The order in which these happen all depend on the company, and often some of these steps won't happen at all, so please take it as a very rough guide.

1. A screening call with HR to get to know each other
2. Face-to-face meeting with the hiring manager
3. Several face-to-face meetings with stakeholders and potentially, the CEO
4. Group / panel interview, in some cases
5. Team dinner/drinks
6. Salary and start date negotiation
7. Offer (written/verbal)
8. Deadline to sign offer (usually 1-2 weeks)

What They Will Ask You In the Interview

Here are a list of questions that are likely to be asked in some form or another. Having read the previous chapters, many of these you should be able to answer by now. Of course, many of these will be company and industry specific, so you'll need to do specific research for each recruitment firm you apply to.

What do you know about the recruitment industry? Do you understand the difference between contingency and retained search? (chapter 1!)
What do you know about our company? Who are our competitors? What industry do we focus on?
Why are you interested in recruitment?
Why do you wake up in the morning?
How would you find a new client from scratch?
Do you have any sales experience? If not, what traits do you have that you think are transferable to sales? (Tenacity, persistence, hard work, resilience to emotional stress)
You don't have any experience in recruitment, so what steps will you take to learn about our industry and reduce the learning curve?
How do you find candidates in recruitment?
How do you find clients in recruitment?
Do you know how the recruitment business model works? Can you explain it to me?
What is your long-term motivation for staying in Japan? Why are you here?
What was your biggest achievement thus far?
What was your biggest failure thus far?
Give me an example when you had to complete something under a deadline or under pressure.
How do you feel about KPIs/targets?

What skill sets do you have that would contribute to the job?

Do you have any sales experience? If so, what were your targets?

"You should never judge a book by its cover." Give me three reasons why you agree and three reasons why you disagree with that statement.

What questions do you have for me?

The last one is particularly important. Taking some time to research the company a drafting a few, well thought out, questions about the company, the role or their plans for the future will show the interviewer that you have put some effort into finding out about them and are purposeful in your approach.

It's tempting to write out a long script to answer all of these questions. You can do this, but don't memorize it, because you'll run the risk of panicking in the interview and forgetting. Some of these are meant to assess whether you think on your feet, so there's probably little point in trying to prepare too many answers.

Rather than preparing 20 answers to 20 questions, my suggestion is to prepare three or four very detailed examples **from which you can draw several ideas.** An example of your biggest achievement could also include sub-examples for a tight deadline, teamwork, and other lessons you learned during that achievement. This is best done using the STAR method.

The Best Way to Answer Questions: STAR
Use The STAR Interview Method: Situation, Task, Action, Result.

When AirBnB started, there were just a couple of guys running it with practically no money and no product, trying to build something on the unprecedented idea of "opening up and sharing your home with others," going against centuries of tradition. How did they raise millions of dollars in venture capital funding and expand to 50+ countries in just 5 years without owning any physical assets? How does *any* startup raise funding? It takes a very careful and well-orated story to convince someone that your idea, which is just an idea at this point, is going to make them millions of dollars in the future. They're betting on a story.

Stories have taught us much of what we know about the world. For example, how do you know what police work looks like? What's the process for a criminal investigation or court hearing? We've seen all of these on fictional shows like *CSI or Dexter*. What would we know about the life of poor Indian children living in the slums or life in Afghanistan, if it weren't for books like *Slumdog Millionaire* and *The Kite Runner*? Books, movies, tv shows, and videos shape our view of the world, regardless of how accurate or inaccurate they may really be.

The point is that stories have a powerful sculpting power over our imaginations and beliefs. It has been proven that stories can influence our personality and change our opinions.

What is STAR?

STAR is a way to answer questions. It's a way to *structure* your examples in an interview. It's also an outline for telling an effective story, and, I believe, it's the *one thing* that's going to knock it out of the park for you. When asked any question like "tell me about a time when..." or "what was your biggest achievement/failure," or basically any questions that requires you to tell some sort of story or provide an example, you can use the STAR method. This method will help you structure any of your responses to sound logical, concise, and descriptive.

There are four steps:

S - define the situation. Where were you and what specific situation or activity were you involved in? *(I was in charge of event planning for our yearly fundraiser. One week before our event, our venue canceled on us.")*

T - define the task. What was required of you and what was your responsibility? Focus on where *you* were specifically. *(It was my job to find a new venue as soon as possible.)*

A - actions. What specific actions did you take to address the problem? Who else was involved? *(I contacted 100 venues with the help of an intern)*

R - result - highlight the end result. Did you achieve the goal? Or not? What was the value of the result? Can you talk about it in terms of percentage/monetary value? What did you learn from it? *(We found a new venue that was actually $300 cheaper and the event was a success. We got lucky. But I also learned that you should always have a plan B.)*

There are many companies who explicitly recommend that you use STAR as the best prep tool to nail their interviews. Other companies don't specifically recommend using STAR, but instead indicate they will ask *behavioral interview* questions. The best way to answer behavioral interview questions is with the STAR technique. **Practically all companies use some method of behavioral interviewing.** Behavioral interviewing just means they want to hear stories about your past, which might indicate your ability to do the job you are interviewing for. All of these companies are essentially saying one thing:

"Please, oh please, tell us a good story!"

The importance of being able to tell a story in relation to what you might be doing in the job is one of the best ways that you're going to be able to show that you are capable. Of course, you might have a specific experience or achievement written on your resume that indicates, "Yes, I've done this before." However, it's unlikely that all of the details are spelled out on your resume, so greater *context* is necessary in order to explain the relevance. This is where your storytelling powers comes in.

Like any good story, you will need to start by painting a picture of what happened, where you were, and who were the people involved. This is the *situation*. There will likely be something that is required or expected of you to be done. You have to identify what this is and describe it clearly. This is the *task*. Once you've decided the goal or outcome you would like to achieve, you need to take steps to get there. What steps did you take and why did you take them? That's the *action*. After moving forward with your plan, what happened? Were you successful, and what did you learn? This is the *result*.

Use this as a standard framework to answer questions and it will help you sound more consistent and take a lot of the thinking out of answering, as you already know the general structure in which you're going to answer.

(By the way, I wrote an entire book on the STAR method which you can find on Amazon).

Transferable Skills

My friend — let's call him Daniel — was telling me the story of how he got hired into recruitment. He had finished a round of grueling interviews for an agency recruitment firm in Tokyo. Alot was on the line, as his visa was expiring and he needed work. If he got the offer, this job would mark the transition from English teaching into the world of sales; that is, actually working for a *company*.

Daniel enjoyed his interactions with all of the people he'd met so far and the feedback was positive from both ends—he was feeling rather hopeful that he'd get the job. He just had to get through one more round. The final interview was with the director of the company. He was a no-BS kind of guy who had those eyes that pierce straight through you. Even if you weren't hiding anything, it felt like you were confessing. Some might call this scary, others call it "having presence."

It didn't start off very well. The director's face showed little sign of emotion. Not impressed, not disappointed—uncertainty was the worst. He asked Daniel questions about his sales experience, of which he had none. He framed the question a few different ways, but any way he spun it, there was no getting past the fact that Daniel had zero sales experience; he had been an English teacher for the past 5 years in some middle-of-nowhere town in rural Japan.

There were some awkward silences that felt like they were going on for an eternity. Only 10 minutes had gone by. *Sweat dripped.* Eventually, the meeting felt like it was coming to an end. The problem was that it was supposed to last 30 minutes, but the director was getting ready to wrap things up after only 15. Never a good sign.

Things were going downhill fast, and Daniel felt like he'd screwed up his last shot at getting the job. But then, at the very last minute, the God of Mercy woke up from his cosmic siesta and swooped down to readjust the course of history.

As a final question to wind things down, the director asked Daniel about extracurricular activities, hobbies, and what he did in his spare time (not an uncommon question in Japan). Daniel brought up his hobby: reselling products on eBay. For the first time, the director actually seemed intrigued.

"Tell me more."

Daniel had started reselling Playstation 2's on eBay a few years back when he started his English teaching job. H bought them in Japan and resold them in England where he lived before, taking advantage of the arbitrage opportunity. He turned it into a profitable business, netting several thousand USD/month. He did his own sales, marketing, and customer service. He learned how to use pivot tables on Excel and did all of the inventory management himself. It was essentially a one-man business that he was running from his room while he had a full time job.

"That sure as hell sounds a lot like recruitment."

There were so many parallels to recruitment — taking initiative, handling customers, managing your own time, etc. Why on earth had Daniel not brought it up previously? Why didn't he put it on his resume? Perhaps a lack of interview know-how up to that point left him clueless as to the obvious connection of transferable skills. In any case, he was hired the next day.

Now, not everyone trying to transition into a completely new industry can talk about the online business they started on the side when interviewing with companies. However, many will inevitably bump into one obvious, glaring fact: you have zero sales experience. The best way to get past this is to find parallels between *anything* in your life. First, answer the following three questions; write down whatever comes to mind.

- *What do other people tell you that you're good at?*
- *What could you do (or talk about) all day and never get tired of?*
- *What have you done in the past that you get compliments on?*

Next, review the lists in the following five categories and underline all the skills you have. Then go back and circle the 10 underlined skills you would enjoy using most. These are all skills that are to some degree used in recruitment, so you'll be able to use them as examples during your interview. Write these top 10 skills down, then write a brief example of how you've demonstrated each skill in a job, class, internship, or extracurricular activity.

Human Relations
Counseling
Advocating for a cause/idea

Coaching
Motivating others around you
Empathizing
Active listening
Genuine curiosity

Planning/Research
Brainstorming ideas
Consuming a large amount of information and synthesizing
Thinking visually
Designing programs
Anticipating consequences of actions having expertise of knowledge in X topic
Improvising

Communication
Breaking down complex problems
Speeches, presentations
Writing effectively
Facilitating discussions
Working in a team setting
Thinking on your feet
Persuading
Summarizing
Networking

Organization
Planning events
Managing your time during a busy schedule

Solving problems
Coming up with new ideas from scratch
Coordinating tasks
Giving directions
Resolving conflicts
Setting priorities
Meeting deadlines

Life
Dealing with a big failure
Bouncing back from rejection/failure
Seeing improvement over the long term
Motivation through tough times
Risk taking/dealing with uncertainty

The rule of 3s

When answering questions I recommend using the rule of 3s, like listing 3 things that qualify you. No more and no less. Thomas Jefferson and Steve Jobs used this technique, so it's probably a good one to try out. There's something about listing things in 3s that makes it very powerful.

Your Greatest Weakness

When interviewers ask about your greatest weakness, the biggest mistake would be to respond with some cookie-cutter answer like *"my greatest weakness is that I am a perfectionist"* or *"I work too hard."* Those answers are just sucking up. Interviewers weren't born yesterday and are not going to fall for the "spin that slightly negative thing into a really positive thing" approach because it sounds too rehearsed and insincere. Unfortunately, most people make this mistake. Instead of having the positive impact they were expecting, it ends up hurting them in the interview.

Companies want to hear a *real* weakness. They want to know the real you so that they can have a full picture of what makes you tick. They also want to test if you are self aware enough to be able to identify areas of improvement in yourself. I've experienced this on both sides of the interview table. I remember interviewing someone once and asking her this question. She responded with something fluffy that didn't sound like a weakness at all. I pressed her but she couldn't come up with anything else. This was a deal breaker for me because it showed a lack of self-reflection and humility about one's own shortcomings.

On the other side of the table, when I was an interviewee asked about my weaknesses, it was an easy (but painful) question to answer. How do I know my own weaknesses? I know them because when I look back at all of the big mistakes, money lost, hurt, and tragedies that could have been avoided in my personal and professional life, 80% of the time they come back to lack of attention to detail. It's still something I struggle with and strive to improve upon.

If you put Lebron and Einstein on a basketball court, would you think any less of Einstein because of his subpar basketball skills? I don't think so. You would probably appreciate that both have very different strengths and weaknesses. The way to talk about weaknesses then is to really just fess up. If you have issues giving feedback, then talk about that and give an example. If your weakness is a tendency to get distracted easily, show how this had a negative impact in your actual work. Don't sugarcoat it and don't pretend like the problem is gone. Explain what steps you take to mitigate it but admit that it's still something you're working on.

Former Navy Seal and author Jocko Willink talks about this in his book, *Extreme Ownership*. He points out that 99.9% of failure in the Navy Seals has nothing to do with their physical skills or mental toughness.

> *"What makes a person fail as a leader is that they are not humble enough to accept responsibility for their mistakes...[...] Ego drive can be good and pushes people to do better. Where ego becomes the enemy is when it becomes too big. They can't take criticism and they can't take ownership when mistakes happen, so*

they point fingers at other people. With ownership you take control of your ego and take responsibility for your actions."

Take full ownership of your weaknesses, flaws, and shortcomings. Weaknesses are not positive things. They suck, or else we wouldn't call them weaknesses. We realize we may never truly turn them into strengths, but we are aware of them and are working to improve them, and that's okay.

How to Manage the Perception of "Flight Risk"

If you're fresh off the boat in Japan, haven't lived here, or aren't here yet, then you'll inevitably be asked the question, "Why do you want to work in Japan?" How you answer this question can make it or break it for you. One of the biggest fears companies have when hiring foreigners is the possibility of a "flight risk." When we had the Fukushima earthquake, tsunami, and nuclear meltdown, thousands of foreigners fled Japan. People referred to them not as gaijin, but as "flyjin."

Many of them packed up their bags without telling their landlords and just went back to their countries. Just like that. Real estate agencies couldn't reach many of them and it all left a pretty bad taste in their mouths, not to mention the negative financial repercussions. The way they saw it: they got screwed over by foreigners, and they basically did. Apart from that black swan event,

English teachers in Japan or those who are here on expat assignments tend to leave pretty quickly anyway. A majority, something like 97% of them, leave within the first couple of years. My study abroad university class was representative of this, and of the dozens of friends I made in Tokyo, almost none of them decided to stay in Japan afterwards and have since moved back to their home countries.

If companies believe you have a good chance of leaving the country, are they really going to invest all of this time and money to train and hire you when you might be gone in a year?

This impacts how companies hire foreigners in Japan in a number of ways (*generally speaking*):

1. Companies will tend to favor those who are Japanese or foreigners who've been in Japan a long time.
2. Companies will also tend to favor those who speak Japanese, because it means they know how to navigate the country more smoothly.
3. It makes it more difficult for you to get a non 'standard foreigner job' (not teaching English) as companies feel like they're taking a big gamble.

In particular, I find that there's a not-so-subtle sexism that also exists among some recruitment companies. The image is that non-Japanese women, specifically Western women, will have a harder time working in recruitment in Japan. The "logic" behind this is that foreign women are at a significant disadvantage. They have to deal with the already sexist nature of Japanese business, a largely male-dominated recruitment industry, *and* the fact that they are a foreigner. And, if they don't speak the language, it's even trickier. It can't get much worse than that.

I've had conversations with foreign female colleagues who've both succeeded and failed in recruitment in Japan, and there's certainly some truth to this. That said, I've seen plenty of very successful female recruiters in Japan. It's unfortunate when companies take this default mindset to hiring, as it turns out being a largely self-fulfilling prophecy and, moreover, sexist. While there are some extra challenges a female recruiter might face, in the end, all of this puts you in a slightly awkward and defensive position. You have to basically prove that you're committed to staying in Japan and that you're "tough enough" to work in the recruitment industry. You can do this in a few ways, and it applies to both men and women.

#1 Show Commitment

Here are some very specific things you can do that will show your commitment:

Longevity. *Tell them you are committed to stay in Japan for at least 5 years.* In reality, you might leave a lot sooner. Whatever. It doesn't matter. Waffling around the question, "Hmm, maybe 2-3 years or so" isn't going to do it for them. Japanese companies, in particular, are still tainted by the lifetime employment system so anything less than 5 years seems like an extremely short stint to them.

Goals. *What are your short- and mid-term goals? Can you map them out for the company you are meeting with in a logical way?* When I moved to Japan, I had a couple of simple goals. One, gain a strong network in the Japanese tech community. Two, gain management experience. The mid term-goal was to establish a startup company after I quit. I told all of the companies I was interviewing with it would take me at minimum 4-5 years to do that in Japan. People liked hearing that I had goals tied to Japan but also personal goals not all related to Japan. Check out the book The ONE Thing that can help you better articulate your goals.

Language study. *Get some Japanese under your belt.* If you enroll in a 3-6+ month language study, whether in our outside of Japan, you're showing that you have an interest in the language/culture. Even if you never become fluent, it's going to be helpful. Ideally, studying here for 6 months to 1 year is going to solidify you as someone who is invested. Most of all, show enthusiasm for the culture/language.

Community. *What do you enjoy? Tennis, pottery, yabusame horse archery, drinking Aomori sake?* You can join many clubs, meet-ups, and various organizations to integrate yourself into the community. Getting involved in a local community group and activity and dedicating any amount of time is going to show that you're integrated to a deeper level. It's not going to be the deciding factor for them, but it helps.

Husband/Wife/Boyfriend/Girlfriend. If you just started dating someone yesterday, this might not be as pertinent. However, companies definitely take into account if you have a partner here to whom you're committed (and if you're married to a Japanese person, the visa no longer becomes an issue).

Internships. Finding a free or paid internship in Japan while you're also studying in Japan is a great way to expose yourself. I know many people who've interned or worked part time, and because they were able to do an outstanding job in a short space of time, the company offered them a full-time job. Consider this as an option, as it's much better than having no job at all, and it gives you the benefit of studying Japanese on the side while you intern.

Other jobs. If you can't land your dream job in Japan it makes sense to do something else for a few months to build your street credit, whether that's English teaching, recruitment, or whatever else. Simply spending 6-12 months in Japan will establish enough credibility for you to get your foot in the door and then re-interview.

#2 Show Humility and Cultural Sensitivity

How can you tell if a foreigner has been living in Japan for a while? By the way in which they communicate with Japanese people. They are usually not extremely boisterous or commanding in the conversation. They listen, make minimal hand gestures, and are generally less aggressive in their communication style. I've spoken with many foreigners, from designers to CEOs, who came to Japan and had to really tone down their usual communication style. When in Rome...

What does this mean, realistically? When you are in an interview, it means the following:

- *Listening before you speak.* Also, not being too assertive without first having asked lots of questions. "Getting shit done" often means following directions, not necessarily being proactive to come up with a 100 new ideas.
- *Be careful about being overconfident.* Saying something like, "I can totally adapt to Japanese culture in a few months" probably is going to be hard to believe. Be realistic about the challenges and come up with a game plan (integrating yourself into the society and learning the language). Being super adaptable to any and every situation is a cliche and *not* realistic. You will face a struggle and encounter things that take time to learn. The more humble you are about this the better.

When you barge into an interview room throwing your hands around and explaining how interested you are in working in Japan (or the opposite, not having any good reasons), the typical Japanese interviewer is going to be quite concerned.

Jeffrey Goldman describes his approach to hiring talent for his company in Japan:

> *"All of my coworkers are Japanese and non-native speakers of English. We don't want a big boisterous personality with tons of great ideas and questions about how each part of the company is run. At this stage in our lifecycle, we need people who can get things done without asking questions each step of the way. We look for self-starters who will Google things and figure them out for themselves.*
>
> *I sat in on an interview with a foreigner once who was a really qualified candidate for the position he was applying for. His resume was super impressive and he had an amazing portfolio. Afterwards, I spoke with my teammate, and she immediately rejected him as a possible candidate because she didn't think he'd be able to follow directions and do the work we actually needed done, which is generally not the most glamorous or creative tasks.*
>
> *So before applying to a company, ask yourself if you're the right kind of person for their stage of growth. Do you need a higher salary or are you willing to trade*

certain perks for the opportunity to work in Japan?"

Another key word here is practicing *humility*. Often, it's misconstrued as passiveness, what you're really witnessing is the Japanese tendency not to get all up in your business and assert their dominance or intelligence or offer advice. Assertiveness will be mistaken for arrogance in many cases, so that's a big one I would watch out for.

The best way around overcoming our own cultural tendencies to behave and act in a certain way (i.e., learning a new behavior in a new culture) is to observe people in the culture we're trying to learn about. That means you should meet with and speak to lots of Japanese people. Observe their mannerisms, when they choose to speak, and how they speak about certain topics. Rochelle Kopp has written some great books on Japanese business. The other part of this is simply learning the language, even if it's only at a basic level. When you start learning Japanese, you'll start thinking differently.

To summarize:
1. Many companies in Japan will think you're a flight risk if you're just getting here.
2. By showing you're committed to Japan through your actions, you can convince them otherwise.
3. Japanese culture is different and you'll have to adapt your interview style. The best way to do

this is to stay humble, observe Japanese people, and then adapt to their communication style.

If you can nail down these two basic ideas then you'll be a step ahead of most people.

Great Questions *You* Should be Asking the Interviewer

Interviews go both ways— *you* are also interviewing the company, not just getting interviewed. Naturally, you should get a lot of information before making a decision to join, but I've found that most people prepare only a handful of questions. Are you going to make a life decision (your career) by only asking five questions? If you're buying a house or a car, would you only ask five questions before deciding? I hope not, and interviewing for a job is no different.

Also, having great questions shows that you've done your research and are genuinely curious about the business. This is your chance to stand out. With that in mind, I always recommend having at least 10-15 questions prepared. I know it sounds like a lot, but you can save some of the questions for other interviews. You might have questions other than the ones on my list below, which you should. However, beware of the "bad question." A bad question is simply this: *If you can find the answer on Google, then it's a bad question.* You want to ask questions that are insightful and that cannot be readily found online. Otherwise, it looks like you haven't done your homework.

Here are some examples of specific questions to ask that will help to reveal important information you will need to make a decision about investing in a career with the company and hopefully start a conversation.

- Why did you choose recruitment, and what's your story? *(This is a great probing question to understand that person's motives, recruiters love to hear themselves talk...like all people).*
- What is the typical day like for one of your recruitment consultants?
- What are your company's biggest pain points (challenges) right now?
- How do the first 3 months look like on the job? What can I expect? Where do most people screw up?
- What are the specific targets and KPIs on a weekly, monthly, quarterly and yearly basis? How are these measured and kept track off? Is there a weekly catch up to discuss these? How are these decided?
- How would you describe your organizational culture? What specific examples do you have that exemplify these aspects of your culture?
- What makes a recruiter successful at your firm, specifically? How is it different than being a recruiter at a different firm?
- Who are your candidates and what skills do they have? Are they mostly Japanese or foreign? What's the percentage breakdown?

- Who are your top clients? Do they speak English, Japanese mostly (or other languages)? Are there any specific clients with whom I could start working immediately? What team would I be on?
- What is the growth trajectory and targets for promotion in this position? What was the fastest someone has been promoted? What was the slowest?
- What CRM system do you use? *(CRM means customer-relationship-management, and is the software you will be using to input and record information internally. Salesforce is a popular one).*
- What are the average fees for your consultants? Or what is the average billing of a good consultant at your firm? What does the top biller make in terms of revenue (not salary)? *(This is a great question because it shows that you are both number driven and business minded)*
- What is your compensation structure? How and when is the bonus paid exactly? What percentage of the fee goes to bonus? *(again, you don't want to ask this during the first interview. I would specifically wait for the client to bring this up. When they do, you know it's usually a good sign that they're interested in moving things forward)*
- What is your training program like? How long does it last?
- Do you have a probationary period, and how

long is it? *(A probationary period is anywhere from 3-6 months, where you have certain "newbie" goals that are set out for you until you get up to speed in the company. This is normal for most companies.)*
- To the hiring manager (your future boss): What is your management style? How has it changed over time?
- To the CEO: What is your vision for the company? Why did you join/start the company? What big challenges are you facing now? What's the most important thing you're working on right now? Here's a few more.
- Mr. Interviewer, do you have any lingering concerns or questions about my fit for the job, or any hesitations about me for the job? *(This is a great one that most people don't ask, as it gives you another shot to squash any lingering doubts they have about you. Ask it at the end of each interview with every single person that you meet)*

The first interview in particular should be reserved for really learning about each other and their business, not about "what's in it for me." There are certain questions that are inappropriate during the first interview. For example, you don't want to ask about salary in the first interview. Don't talk about the start date, ask how late you have to work, or ask how many vacation days you would get. You'll find out all of this as you talk to more people. This may seem obvious to some people, but when you've just gotten to Japan (especially if it's your first job), or if you haven't interviewed in a while, it's easy to slip up with a basic error like this.

Lastly, make sure to bring a notebook and take notes during the interview; never show up empty handed. You are unlikely to remember big pieces of the interview because you'll be receiving lots of new information, and you'll want to refer back to your notes in case you have questions later on. Also, this a simple yet effective way to show the company that you care enough to write down what they're saying.

The Flipside of KPIs

*"A **Key Performance Indicator** (KPI) is a measurable value that demonstrates how effectively a company is achieving key business objectives. Organizations use key performance indicators at multiple levels to evaluate their success at reaching targets. High-level KPIs may focus on the overall performance of the enterprise, while low-level KPIs may focus on processes or employees in departments such as sales, marketing or a call center." - Klipfolio*

You will likely run into some companies that are more "strict" on KPIs than others. The specific KPIs are important to consider because how you are measured will influence your behavior, stress levels, and ultimate success. If the company has no KPIs and just lets everyone "do their thing," this will make it difficult for you to progress if you're new to the industry because you've had minimal training; in other words, KPIs are especially useful when you're starting out.

However, they can also be restricting, and don't always paint a full picture. Speaking from my own experience, historically, KPIs provided a sense of how employees were doing on the job. This made it easier for us to forecast performance for periods of weeks/months. While this is certainly true, as I got **better** at the job I realized this logic fell apart. How was I able to *ignore* these indicators myself, but still exceed in my results?

Simply put, there were factors you couldn't measure such as…

- The quality of relationships I had built, which made me more effective, despite my "low" numbers.
- My intuition about certain deals (how likely I was to conclude the placement) that allowed me to take an 80/20 approach—being confident about *where* to focus my time.
- My brand in the industry that had developed from customer service + tenure. Meaning clients came to me, and I had to put in less legwork.

Ignoring my targets was seen as okay, since I was hitting my revenue target. Ironically, focusing on the main target (revenue) instead of daily targets reduced my stress and decreased my admin time, which freed up more time for actual sales activity.

While I had to start with KPIs, I eventually developed the intuition to graduate from them.

I recognize certain numbers are worth following, some indicators are better than others, and it can take time to build the 'intangible' sales skills I described. But this led me to consider that perhaps there's less power to the numbers than was being touted — or perhaps the qualities of success were more opaque and non-measurable.

This is not to say we should throw away KPIs or that you should be overly cautious about them when interviewing with recruitment firms; most firms will have them. Rather, you should be asking the questions, "How are these KPIs determined? How flexible are these KPIs as I become more senior in the organization?" There should be flexibility from the company, but if not, then that's a warning sign.

> *"Measure what you can, evaluate what you measure, and appreciate that you cannot measure the vast majority of what you do."*
> **—Ed Catmull, President of Walt Disney and Pixar**

CHAPTER 6

HOW TO NAIL THE ROLE PLAY INTERVIEWS

If you got excited when you saw the classic "sell me this pen" scene in *Wolf of Wall Street* and thought *hey, I could do that!* then you'll probably enjoy the role-play section of the interviews. If not, then that's okay because you won't be selling too many pens in a recruitment job anyways.

Frankly, I haven't been asked to sell a pen before (in an interview setting), but you *will* be put on the spot and be expected to come up with a convincing sales pitch. I'll give you a hint to a successful pitch: **rather than selling by pushing your ideas/information/pitch down someone's throat, always start by asking a question and establish rapport; then the rest will flow a lot easier.**

The basics of most effective pitches are as follows:

1. Introduce yourself.
2. Ask questions.
3. Tell a story, not a sales pitch.
4. Listen.
5. Don't hurry, and don't push.

In a recruitment scenario you'll be asked to participate in a group interview or a role play where they place you in various real-life scenarios which you would be likely to encounter as a recruiter to play through. The interview role plays and group interview are practical scenarios and usually take place in a large meeting room at their office. They are not expecting you to ace these interviews or have the perfect answers, particularly if you don't have recruitment experience. They're more interested to see how quickly you can react, the decisions you make, and your thinking process. In some ways, it's a good corollary for what you'd actually be doing in the job. Thus, while it's natural to be nervous, if you absolutely hate this part of the interview, then that might be a sign that it's not the right career for you.

The first time I had to do the role plays, I was pretty bad. I choked and froze a few times, and it was embarrassing. Even when I did get a few job offers and started work, I would still get quite nervous sometimes, and, in reality, never became the "smooth talking sales guy," but I was efficient and pushed through. Understand that it is unlikely that you're going to be able to perform these roleplays and on the job tasks smoothly at first, as there's always some nerves when you're placed on the spot, and in unfamiliar territory. I wouldn't worry so much about being smooth or overthinking the best approach. Rather, showing enthusiasm and a willingness to jump in head first into the role play and just give it a shot is going to be seen more favorably than being the slickest talker.

The four basic scenarios you will likely come across are listed as follows.

A summary of the different role plays:

1. New business development calls
2. Headhunting calls/cold-calling a candidate
3. New client meetings with hiring manager
4. Pitching/introducing a job to a potential candidate

Let's explore what they are really looking for and how to approach them.

#1 New Business Development (finding new clients).

How do you get leads? How do you find and develop new clients from scratch? The goal of this role play (or sometimes it's in the form of a one-on-one question) is usually to cold-call a new client, or to find out which companies are hiring. Let me set the context. Let's say that all you have in front of you is the Internet and a phone. How do you start recruiting? How do you get clients? How do you find people looking for a job? What steps do you need to take?

Before you find candidates, you have to find clients who are hiring. Otherwise, you have nothing to offer the candidates. One of the simplest ways to find a job opening would be to look under "jobs" on LinkedIn. Or any job board. Or any company page under the "jobs section." You'll see that Amazon is hiring for a marketing manager, for example.

Another way to find out for what jobs companies are hiring is to *ask candidates where they are interviewing.* If you know that Bob is interviewing at Apple for a engineering job, you, therefore, know that Apple is hiring for that job. The information that there's a job in the market is called a "lead." It's as simple as that. You can now follow up on this lead, and the next action will be to contact a hiring manager at Amazon, with the intent of working with them. The best way is to call the company directly. Quick tip — if you type in the number extension "03-" into Google, followed by the company name in Japan, then it will usually bring up the companies phone number at the very top.

We don't want to talk to HR because they're usually not the decision makers. HR people are known as "gatekeepers" because they are often the ones who block you from talking to someone of authority in the company. They often want to protect the status quo and don't want to work with more recruitment agents. To get around this, we want to talk to a manager in charge of hiring. If we have a "lead" for a marketing manager job, most likely, the person in charge is the person one step up, the marketing director. If it's a sales manager, then we contact the sales director. And so on.

Now that we have the context, in the actual role play you might be asked, "How do you find leads?" The simple answers are:

- Get leads from candidates who are interviewing at X company (ask candidates directly if they are interviewing anywhere).
- Social Media — Linkedin, Twitter, Facebook, Wantedly
- Jobs pages of companies (online job boards)
- Backfill jobs. For example, if you know that John recently quit his job as a sales manager at Microsoft, then you know Microsoft probably needs to hire another sales manager as John's replacement or "backfill."

How do you get in touch with the companies/hiring managers? Phone. Email. Website directly. Go and meet them at an event. Ask to be introduced via a mutual connection. If you are asked to make an imaginary phone call to a prospective client, the goal is to *get a meeting*.

Here's one of my favorite cold calling scripts provided by *Brandon Redlinger, Head of Growth at PersistIQ,* slightly modified with my own comments.

1. **Get their attention by using their name.** Start off my saying "Hi, ____," in a warm and welcoming tone, then proceed directly to Step 2. Notice I didn't say, "Hi, ____, how are you today?" because it gives your prospect a chance to jump in and disrupt your flow. Cold calls are all about taking control in the beginning.
2. **Identify yourself.** "My name is Brandon with PersistIQ." This is pretty straightforward — you need to tell them who you are.
3. **Tell them why you're calling.** "The reason I'm calling is to get some time on your calendar." Diving right in demonstrates that you're a professional. Save the small talk for your follow-up calls after you've already built the relationship.
4. **Build a bridge and create a hook.** This statement connects the reason you're calling with why they should care. "I just noticed on your site that

you're hiring 10 new sales reps this quarter. I've actually spoken to two great sales candidates from X company (their competitor, hopefully), and they're quite interested in your firm. I'd love to send over their resumes." By showing that you have qualified candidates (even if you don't you can find them!), it actually gives you credibility, and it gives you a further incentive to start contacting candidates for the job.

5. **Ask for what you want and shut up.** "I thought the best place to start is to schedule a meeting to learn about your outbound sales challenges and goals, and I can bring along the resumes. Do you have time Wednesday or Thursday afternoon around 10 a.m.?" Ultimately, our goal is to set meetings with prospects because we're calling on a more targeted list. However, if you're calling on a less qualified list, then you might ask for a piece of information that qualifies the lead.

Here are links to a few more good scripts that you can use.

- https://www.slideshare.net/TopEchelon/cold-calling-scripts-for-recruiters
- https://blog.pipedrive.com/2016/05/cold-calling-scripts/
- http://recruitloop.com/blog/recruiter-tips-its-time-to-lose-the-script/

#2 Headhunting: Cold-calling new candidates.

Headhunting means that you're calling or contacting someone you don't know, and trying to get a meeting with them because they could be a strong candidate. You could be asked to role play, or even do a live call. The best candidates are *not* looking for jobs, so why would they meet with you? What's your value to them as a recruiter?

1. You can provide them with market information (what the market trends are).
2. You can give them career advice that they would not get access to otherwise.
3. Even if they're not looking for a new job, you can learn about what they want to do, what their long term goals are (their "dream job"), and stay in touch with them so that when you do come across that dream job, you can reach out.
4. You can connect them to valuable business partners.

If you're asked to make an imaginary phone call to a prospective candidate, remember that the goal is to *get a meeting*. If you can't get a meeting with someone, *get their email*. You don't want to hang up the phone empty handed. There are tons of great scripts online that you can use to prepare for these sorts of phone calls, but the simple key points to remember about cold-calling are as follows:

- Cut to the chase from the start. "We've never spoken before, but I'm a recruiter at X Recruitment Company."
- Make them feel special. "Your name was recommended to me by someone in the industry" (if they ask who, tell them that you have to keep their names confidential out of respect) or "I came across your profile on LinkedIn and was impressed with X part of your career."
- Tell them why you're calling. "A client of mine in the X industry (be specific, but don't say the name of the company) is looking for someone with your skills and I wanted to share an overview of the role with you. Honestly, I don't know if it's a match for you or what you want to do in your career, but I, at least, wanted to share the information and start a conversation with you.
- Set a meeting. "I am in your area, Roppongi (find out where their office is so you can sound smoother and familiar), this Thursday afternoon, do you have time for a brief, casual coffee?

Inevitably, some people will tell you that they're not interested in finding a job right now, which is fine. Your response is simply that you speak to lots of people who are not actively looking for jobs, and, in fact, most people you speak to just meet you to gather information about the job market and career prospects. Keep a casual tone. If they still say no, then at least get their email address and follow up with an email restating what you said on the phone, as it's possible you caught them at an awkward time calling.

Here are a few more:

- https://theundercoverrecruiter.com/cold-calls/
- https://www.topechelon.com/blog/recruiter-training/8-scripts-that-recruiters-can-use-to-cold-call-candidates/
- http://iheadhunter.blogspot.jp/2011/02/5-chalices-script-to-increase-candidate.html
- http://www.recruitingblogs.com/profiles/blogs/headhunting-10-top-tips-for-making-more-successful-calls
- http://theundercoverrecruiter.com/cold-calls/

It's easy to memorize a script, but more importantly, keep in mind the above goals when you're making the call — that's what's important. Alternatively, nowadays, people just email or use LinkedIn to get in touch, but the same rules apply.

#3 Client Meeting : Conducting a new meeting with a prospective client.

The scenario: you're a consultant and you're meeting with a client for the first time to discuss the details of a job opening. So, let's say you're meeting with Amazon for the first time to discuss helping them fill a marketing manager position. This can be one of the most challenging role plays because unless you've done the job, it's hard to put yourself in the shoes of a recruiter. Basically, they're asking you to conduct a mock client meeting.

The goal for you in this sort of role play is to get as much *relevant* information about the client as possible. Relevant means that it's information that you can then use to give prospective candidates an overview of the vacancy, in order to generate their interest in the job. In this role play, you'll usually receive a job description "Amazon: marketing manager" and have 10 minutes to look at it and prepare questions for the hiring manager. The job description might look like this.

Job Description

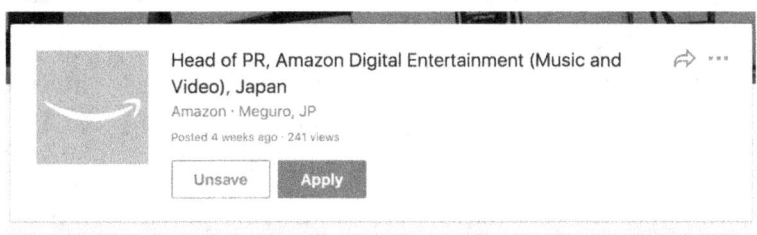

In less than 3 years since their Japan launches, Amazon's digital video & music services, Prime Video & Amazon Music, are changing the way people consume and enjoy entertainment. Our mission is to build the widest selection of digital video and music content and make it trivially easy for customers to enjoy wherever and whenever they want.

As Senior PR Manager, you will be asked to develop, execute and oversee strategic communications programs and events designed to support the Prime Video and Amazon Music businesses and their rapid growth in Japan. You will be relied upon as a communication advisor to Amazon's senior business leaders both in Japan and in the U.S. You will be responsible for the proactive communication of our streaming video and music services and promotion of our popular Prime Original series and exclusive content across both video and music, and the local execution for regional and global campaigns and executions. The right candidate should have 10+ years of experience in public relations, preferably in business-to-consumer in-house or at a PR agency.

To succeed in this role, you must have extraordinarily high judgement, strong ownership, energy, creativity, high standards for yourself and others, and Japanese and English writing and verbal skills. You must be willing to think big and long-term, without forgetting to manage the short-term, and be flexible to adapt and deal with ambiguity as priorities change.

Key Responsibilities

- Lead Amazon Entertainment's overall communication strategy in Japan that includes external and internal communications
- Plan and execute a strategic communications plan to support the Prime Video and Amazon Music businesses

- Develop and oversee the execution of content publicity campaigns for Prime Video and Amazon Music, at times leveraging talent for press opportunities
- Work closely with leadership across Prime Video and Amazon Music businesses to develop proactive media opportunities and narratives.
- Build and maintain strong relationships with relevant media
- Manage an internal team of PR professionals and external public relations agencies on strategy and day-to-day matters
- Handle issues management
- Effectively represent Amazon as a spokesperson for assigned businesses as necessary
- Collaborate across internal teams and organization to produce effective results
- Keep current on trends, issues and news about both the business and consumer worlds of media/entertainment
- Manage overall budget

Basic Qualifications

- Minimum of 10+ years of experience in public relations, a significant piece of which should be spent on B to C businesses in-house or PR agency, and proven track record
- Experience in managing teams, both internal and external (i.e., PR agencies)

- High-level media contacts across news/business, consumer, tech, and broadcast sectors
- Proactive self-starter and collaborative team player
- Flexibility and adaptability to manage ambiguity as priorities change
- Exhibits ownership and commitment to delivering results
- Excellent writing skills: A breadth of writing styles for both internal and external stakeholders. Ability to quickly produce solid communications with limited time (e.g., key messages, talking points, FAQs) both in Japanese and English
- Excellent verbal communications: Ability to communicate clearly and effectively for both internal and external stakeholders both in Japanese and English
- Organized to juggle multiple projects simultaneously while managing essential admin work

Preferred Qualifications

- Bachelor's degree or above
- Experience in the media/entertainment industry
- Strong English oral and written language skills - ability to translate between English and Japanese with an appropriate tone and nuance
- Experience working at a fast-paced, global company and dynamic corporate environment

- Have relentlessly high standards and a high attention to detail
- Thinks big

Company - Amazon Japan G.K.

There is a certain "flow" of a client meeting that's better than others. For example, if you sit down in the meeting and say, "Hello, hiring manager, nice meeting you. So, I saw the job description, so tell me about this job." It sounds very abrupt, unnatural, and transactional. Instead, you want to start with an intro and bigger picture concepts, and then flow smoothly into other questions, just like you would in any conversation - no need to make it overly formal.

Here's a natural flow to follow along with specific questions you can ask the hiring manager:

Introduction and Context: *Introduce yourself, what your company does. Quickly set the context for the meeting by saying that you have several questions prepared, and would like to jump right into things.*

The Company and Business: *How big is the company in terms of people and revenue in Japan? Where is HQ? What is the office culture like? Who are your competitors? What is your business model, and how exactly do you make money?*

The Product: *What is their most profitable product? What are other products they plan to launch? What's the product roadmap? Who are the users? How many users do they have? Is the business (or this part of the business) b2b or b2c?*

The Job: *Why are you looking for this person, is it a new position or a backfill? How will you measure the success of this person (what targets do they have)? What is a typical day look like for this person? Are there any specific goals or projects they would be taking on or working on immediately when they join? What do you expect from them the first 3 months? What is the team atmosphere like? What is the salary structure? What kind of company do you see this person coming from? What are the top three selling points for a candidate to be interested in this job? Do they need to speak English/Japanese? How quickly can get they promoted and what's the career growth/path?*

The Hiring Manager: *What is your background? What is your interview style? What kind of team culture are you trying to build? Why did you join this company?*

*Keep in mind that this role play does not always come up. If it is your first job as a recruiter, many recruitment agencies will not always hire you as a consultant. Sometimes you will start off in "sourcing," as a sourcing manager or a sourcing specialist, also known as candidate sourcing. The difference here is that you would not be interacting with clients directly at least for the first 6-12 months, and your main goal would be finding *candidates,* meaning 90% of your job is spent looking for and talking to job seekers and helping with interview scheduling.

#4 "Pitching a job": introducing a job opportunity to a candidate.

Pitching refers to introducing a job to a candidate. In this role play you will have a job description and your goal will be to tell the candidate about the job, answer any rebuttals, and to convince them to apply for the job. Like a client meeting, there is a good flow and a bad flow to introducing a job. Imagine getting a random phone call from someone saying:

> "Hey John, I have a job opportunity for you at this company. Let me tell you about it. My client Amazon is looking for a marketing...blah blah."

You would probably be very annoyed. They don't know what your needs are, didn't even ask if you would be interested, and are just blabbing on. Not cool, and definitely does not instill a sense of trust or confidence in this person. Instead, you want to develop a more natural flow, not as a sales pitch but as a *conversation*. That means you should be asking questions, and they should be doing most of the talking. Let's apply the 80/20 rule of conversation — they do 80% of the talking and you do 20%. Also, a person responds to stories as we discussed earlier. Instead of blabbing about a bunch of details, turn it into a story format with the person as the main character.

Here's what works:

Introduction: Introduce yourself and ask if they have

time to chat for 5-10 minutes. Don't tell them that you have a specific job opportunity right off the bat but that you want to catch up with them.

Getting to Know Them: You want to build rapport and understand what the person's needs are. *What is your current job, what are your main responsibilities? What does your company do? What are your career goals, what's the career plan? Do you think you can achieve those goals in your current company? Are you up for a promotion soon, and what's the next career step you could take internally? Have you considered external job opportunities, or would you be open to hearing market information? (market information = telling them about what kind of companies are currently hiring in Japan)*

Higher Level Company Description, Tailored to Them: Now that you know what their interests are, you can frame your "pitch" to them. If you know they're interested in working for a larger team, then you can emphasize the team size in your pitch. Start with a description of the person you met, as highlighting that individual's story is more powerful than just information about the company. "I just met with Tanaka san from Amazon yesterday who's been running X department for 2 years now. He's a great guy and we had a good conversation about a new product he is helping to develop. He needs help bringing the product to market..." Talk about the company and then talk about the problem or need that they have. "They don't have anyone to lead their marketing initiative, which is a major issue considering it's their top strategic priority for the year."

At no point did you say, "I have a job opportunity for you" Instead, you actually painted a picture and reason for the job. From there, you can take the conversation in several directions, whether its talking about the job itself or more about the company. The great thing is you don't have to give much details of a job description to get someone interested — people are interested in you, whether or not **you** sound trustworthy and whether or not you're taking the time to listen to them.

Action Point: Never leave the call without an action point. If the person seems very interested in the job, you can easily ask if they'd like you to forward their resume to the hiring manager. If they're not interested, tell them you can follow up by email with more details. Also, you can tell them, "No worries, John; perhaps it's not the right opportunity for you. I'll keep in touch about other opportunities in the future. By the way, do you know anyone in your network who might be interested or capable of doing this sort of job?" Ending with something is always better than nothing.

CHAPTER 7

TIPS FOR SUCCESS

Have conversations, not monologues

Interviews are supposed to be conversations but often end up as two people delivering mini-monologues. In order to avoid this, it's almost always better to intermittently elicit small responses from your interviewer to keep them feeling engaged. The easiest way to understand or clarify if someone got your point, or if they need more context, is to drop in cues such as, *"Does this make sense? Does that answer your question?"*

Often, misunderstandings happen not because you don't get the question but because the interviewer is looking for something in particular but phrased the question poorly. Remember, most interviewers don't have much experience interviewing, so it's your job to help guide the conversation and make sure there are no communication blunders. Where an interviewer may not have considered you a strong candidate from the start, sharing a high-context, relevant story allows you to reveal yourself to them as the 'diamond in the rough.'

3 Common Pitfalls

1. Saying "I don't know"

You're not expected to have all of the answers or have the smoothest interview in the world. However, when you respond, "I don't know" to a question they ask, you fail to show that you can solve problems. You don't need an immediate answer. You can even respond with, *"Let me think about that for a minute; hold on."* There's absolutely nothing wrong with pondering a question, and then answering in a few seconds or couple of minutes. In the worst-case scenario, you can ask to pass on the question and answer it later (our brains are funny; usually an answer will pop into your head after a few minutes when you are not focusing so intensely on trying to find one).

2. The Wrong Reasons for Wanting the Job

Pushiness and desperation are very unattractive in any relationship, particularly in job hunting. If you position yourself as "open to any job" and "really interested in recruitment," then you'll literally be like everyone else who is stepping through the door. While you want to be enthusiastic, you also want to be realistic and specific, as well as take a longer-term outlook. You have goals in your life and in your career, and you know how hard you're willing to work for them (or at least how badly you want them). Sometimes, they can be difficult to articulate to other people, so it requires practice. I recommend being very explicit in your description of your goals, and how you think you can achieve them in this particular job. Be specific.

> *"My 1-year goal is to hone my recruitment and sales skills in the pharmaceutical industry, get promoted, build a network, and save X amount of money to pay off student loans. My 3-year goal is X, and, eventually, in 5 years, I'd like to start my own business. I think X and X in your company are relevant skills that I can acquire to achieve my goals."*

Now, in reality, maybe you leave the company in a year or two. You don't know what the situation will be down the road, and perhaps your goals change over time. But for the sake of interviewing, despite the reality that we're all living in a state of uncertainty to a certain degree, the interviewers want to feel that you're committed, just like any other relationship. As mentioned earlier, your commitment to being and staying in Japan is an important factor.

3. Not preparing and stretching yourself too thin.

You're reading this guide, so you've already got a lot of good information at hand, but you still need to prepare for each interview, all of which will depend on the specifics of the position/company you're applying for. As a recruiter, I've assisted thousands of people and I'm always amazed at how little time people actually take to prepare. Some of this comes down to their overconfidence or just "being too busy."

Interviews aren't a natural skill by any means, so we do have to spend an uncomfortable amount of time preparing for them.

Don't stretch yourself too thin — you shouldn't be interviewing with more than three or four companies at any given time, as we want to focus on creating a high quality impression and make ample time to prepare. Fortunately, you have the flexibility to space out interviews as you please. If you're delaying an interview by 2 weeks or more, that's going to be a red flag that you're not serious, but pushing a schedule by a few days is acceptable. In doing so, you'll be able to juggle multiple interviews without getting flustered. In other words, don't schedule three interviews for three different companies on the same day. This might be counterintuitive to some people who want to be "efficient" and knock them all out at once, but unless you've spent several days preparing, you run the risk of overwhelming yourself. Even with ample preparation, interviews are stressful and draining. You don't want to arrive at your second or third interview for the day mentally and emotionally exhausted, with no energy left to represent yourself in the best possible light. I can't tell you how many candidates have told me they felt the interview went "very well" only to get scathing feedback from the interviewer. We're bad at assessing our own performance and can overestimate our own abilities, especially when it comes to pressured, stressful, and unfamiliar situations.

On top of everything already mentioned, checklists are great tools to use on the day of the interview. I would keep some notes in a small pocket notebook that you can bring with you to the interview and review before stepping into the meeting. It will also come in handy to take notes of what the interviewer is saying. The following is a quick checklist of what you should do ahead of every interview:

- Prepare a quick introduction or "elevator pitch"
- Fully understand their business, industry, business model, clientele, competitors.
- Due diligence of who you will be meeting
- Read through every page on their website, do google searches for any news on the company, look on linkedin at current employees.
- A list of three to four detailed examples, as mentioned above
- Questions for the interviewer, 10-15 at minimum
- Thank you note, handwritten

Setting Yourself Apart from the Crowd

Always write a thank you note/letter/email. You'd be surprised how many people overlook this step. Do this for the hiring manager and for everyone you meet throughout the process. It's great icing on the cake. Sure, people remember first impressions, but they also remember the last feeling that your interaction left them with, very strongly. If it's a handwritten note, even better — 99.999% of people don't do this.

> "I've learned that people will forget what you said, people will forget what you did, but people will never forget how you made them feel." —Maya Angelou

Talk to people who have worked there before. Another simple method is searching for people who previously worked at the company that you're interested in interviewing with. You can find them on LinkedIn, simply search for the company name and then on the right hand column select "previous employer" and it will display people who no longer work there.

Once you reach out to them, you can explain that you're considering applying to the company (or interviewing), and would like to hear about their experience working there. Schedule a 15-20 minute call or just email them with questions you have about the company (what was their experience like, what the culture was like, good/bad points, potential for growth, and all of the other things you'd like to know). This doesn't mean you should base your decision solely on their opinion, and keep in mind they're only one person with their own set of experiences and biases, so use it as just another point of assessment.

Build Rapport and Gain Trust

In the movie *The Talented Mr. Ripley,* Matt Damon heads off to Italy to convince the son of a rich textile owner to return home. Matt Damon studies his interest — jazz — and spends some time listening to jazz records, learning the famous tunes and artists. He does this so he can build trust and rapport, and, in the end, is able to win over the son.

You don't have to learn the favorite sport or genre of music of the hiring manager to gain their trust— that's taking it a bit too far. But you've got a lot of information at your fingertips. Facebook, LinkedIn, and Twitter are freely available tools where you can find information about people. Try to find something in common with the person before you go into the meeting. It can be as simple as learning that the interviewer is a big fan of tennis. Even if you don't play tennis, you could do some quick research and find out that the Wimbledon tournament is next week. That way, when the topic of tennis comes up (it might), you're ready to have something relevant to contribute to the conversation. Any small thing that further connects you and the people you're talking to will strengthen their perception of you.

CHAPTER 8

OFFERS AND SALARY NEGOTIATION

- Salary package breakdown
- Base
- Bonus
- Perks
- Negotiation/Deadlines
- Taxes
- Independent vs. Permanent Employee

Salary Package Breakdown

The compensation in recruitment is going to differ in structure from firm to firm. You'll find that the larger recruitment firms usually have a more stable, reasonable base salary and good bonuses. The small boutique firms, though, can often have structures with much lower bases but high incentive bonuses. In other words, your overall earning potential is higher. But in a smaller firm you'll also usually have to bring your own network, and resources will be more limited, so achieving that upper earning potential might pose a much greater challenge. The general rule of thumb is that if you have zero experience in the recruitment industry in Japan, or any work experience at all, it's best to start with a firm that has a guaranteed base salary so you don't have to worry about putting food on the table.

It consists of the following:

- A guaranteed base salary
- Bonus (quarterly/bi annually/yearly) depending on your performance and/or team/company performance
- Perks (expense account, paid-for trips, prizes, and free stuff)
- Commuting expense (almost always guaranteed)
- Health insurance (kokumin hoken, deducted from monthly salary and required by law)
- Japanese Pension (nenkin, deducted from monthly salary)

You can learn more about Japanese health care and pension below:

http://www.nenkin.go.jp/international/english/healthinsurance/employee.html
http://www.nenkin.go.jp/international/english/nationalpension/nationalpension.html

Base Salary

Starting salaries in recruitment in Japan can be anywhere from 3,000,000 to 4,500,000 yen depending on your level of experience, and they can double, triple and more than quadruple depending on the bonus structures and level of experience. If you are being offered less than that, then you should push back, citing the industry standards, which you can easily find on Glassdoor.

In my first year as a recruiter I was making a 4,000,000 yen base salary, but then I exceeded my targets for two consecutive quarters and was able to double my salary to 8,000,000 yen by the end of the year. Living expenses in Japan aren't cheap, particularly if you're in central Tokyo, and I've found that 3,000,000 per year is really at the lower end of what is acceptable, even if you're single. This should be your absolute minimum, unless you have enough money to cushion you for a few months and have a large bonus component that you're confident in earning in the first year.

Bonus/Commission

Every company will have a different bonus scheme/incentive scheme, so it's your job to find out exactly how much your earning potential is during your first year. More often than not, you won't make a bonus during your first 6 months as you'll be on "probation," or a test/trial period with the company. It's standard to have a clear bonus system where you'll be able to understand how much you would make exactly if you hit your targets. Make sure you're 100% clear on that before joining.

Getting paid in whole or in part on a commission basis (or bonus, same thing) means that your performance and success on the job will have a direct impact on your paycheck. Being paid using a commission structure gives you control over how much you earn during a specific period. In many cases, it offers you unlimited earning potential based on how good you are at what you do and how successful you are. It's important to remember that the *fee* a recruiter charges for a placement isn't exactly the same as the amount of money a recruiter *earns* for making that placement (if they work for a recruiting firm). If you work for a corporate recruitment firm, your fees will count towards your monthly or quarterly revenue target, and your bonus or incentive payment will be based on your performance against that target, just like any other sales job.

You'll encounter companies that have one of three systems: 1) a very clear bonus system (make X revenue and make X bonus), 2) a discretionary bonus, or 3) a draw system. The first is self-explanatory as it will be spelled out in plain English for you in the salary conversation, but the other two warrant some explaining.

A "discretionary" bonus system means that the bonus is paid on a range of factors that aren't always apparent until after you join. These factors could include the number of clients you brought in, the candidates you brought in that *other* recruiters place, your team spirit, and customer service feedback. However, for most recruitment firms, while they say "discretionary," this is ultimately determined 90% by the revenue you bring in directly. To gain more clarity, a good question to ask the recruitment firm is,**"If I achieve my targets for an entire year, what would my estimated earnings be?"**

	Company	Salary Range	About Low	About High
	Recruiter — Intersoftkk India (1 employee salary or estimate)	¥3,422K - ¥3,748K	¥3,422K	¥3,748K
	Recruitment Consultant — PageGroup (2 salaries)	¥4,783K - ¥5,246K	¥4,783K	¥5,246K
	Recruitment Consultant — East West Consulting K.K. (1 employee salary or estimate)	¥3,391K - ¥3,632K	¥3,391K	¥3,632K
	Recruitment Consultant — Robert Walters (1 employee salary or estimate)	¥5,325K - ¥5,736K	¥5,325K	¥5,736K
	Recruiting Manager — Cisco Systems (1 employee salary or estimate)	¥7,691K - ¥8,275K	¥7,691K	¥8,275K
	Recruitment Consultant — Hays (1 employee salary or estimate)	¥3,839K - ¥4,194K	¥3,839K	¥4,194K
	Recruitment Consultant - Monthly — Hays (1 employee salary or estimate)	¥285K - ¥312K	¥285K	¥312K

For example: if you are on a discretionary bonus system, place a candidate and charge a $35,000 fee, you don't get a $35k pay day that month. That revenue goes towards your revenue target, but if you make one and only one $35k placement in a month when your revenue target is $40k, you'll unlikely to be paid a bonus that month. A rule of thumb that seems to work well for recruiters working for recruitment firms is: a recruiter earns (before tax) about 25%-30% of the revenue he generates, per year. Perhaps 90% of this is based on revenue and the 10% is based on customer service results or the number of candidates you brought in during a 3 month period.

So, more specifically, if, as an executive recruiter, you made 15 $25,000 placements in a year and therefore generate $375,000 in revenue or roughly 40,000,000 yen (which is in the range of a good/high achieving recruiter in Japan), you'll hopefully get paid about $130k-$140k, or roughly 14,000,000 yen before tax, depending on the incentive structure negotiated with your employer. This might go up or down a bit in a discretionary system. Either way, a *lot* of work would have gone into making those 15 placements, even if the recruiter makes it look easy.

The second system, an intermediary step between the two, is a pay system called draw against commission or **draw bonus,** which is quite common for the small- to medium-size companies. Draw against commission generally works in the following way: At the beginning of each pay period, you're given a specific amount of money in advance, called a "predetermined draw." This draw is deducted from your commissions at the end of a pay period. When you exceed your sales goal, you're paid a commission, but your draw in the past has been "drawn" or subtracted from this commission. Once you meet or exceed the sales goals, you're paid in straight commission, which is normally more than your draw.

For example: You, the recruiter, accepts draw of $4,000 per month. There is a 3-month period before earning a commission of $24,000 (Approx three permanent placements). The commission paid would be $24,000 - (3 x 4,000) = $12,000, so your benefit would equal the entire $24,000 for 3 months. However, if you fail to meet the sales goals in the future, you're merely paid your predetermined draw amount again and the draw against commission starts over.

Perks

Typical perks in recruitment include an expense account, which means that you'll be given a stipend every month that you can use to wine and dine candidates and clients. Since you'll be out and about meeting people for drinks and dinners, you'll be the one paying for them. You simply save your receipts and are reimbursed at the end of the month. It's a great way to eat nice dinners every day - virtually for free.

Some companies allot a specific limit to your expense account such as 30,000 yen, increasing the limit once you're promoted. You don't typically get any money up front and it's just a matter of being reimbursed, so keep this in mind for your own budgeting purposes. Other firms are a lot more generous, though, and simply say,

"Keep your expenses within reasonable limits." During my first and second years of recruitment, I would spend 30,000 to 40,000 yen in expenses per month. Once I became a manager, these expenses doubled and tripled, as I was engaging with more senior clients and candidates, and had to take out entire teams for celebrations and so forth.

Companies doing business in Japan typically pay the full amount of your daily commute, and some will even pay a portion of your rent if you live extremely close to the office. Other perks include trips, holidays, and incentive prizes that you might win during your time as a recruiter. It's not a huge deciding factor, but it's nice to get free stuff from your company.

Salary Negotiation and Deadlines

When receiving an offer, you might need to negotiate start date or salary. My two biggest tips for this are as follows:

1. **Manage expectations**. Do your best to avoid these discussions by addressing them ahead of time earlier in the interview process. If you know that you need 8 weeks to move jobs or get to Japan, for example, you should be upfront about the timeline and how long it's going to take to transition. This will establish their expectations ahead of time. That way, once they do present you with an offer, there are no surprises.

2. **Negotiate by email as often as you can.** Doing so in person or by phone can be quite awkward, and it's easier to succumb to pressure or your own emotions when you have a lot on the line, especially if you haven't had much experience in negotiation. Remember, you're talking to recruiters who do this for a living. Email back and forth, giving yourself space and time to mull over your choices and priorities, and distancing yourself from aggressive negotiation tactics.

It's common to receive a 1-2-week deadline to accept an offer once you receive it. In reality, this is a totally arbitrary timeline that the company sets, but the reason they do so is so that you don't run off and join another company in the meantime. It's in their best interest. Recruitment requires you to make lots of decisions quickly, so by waffling around for 2 weeks and not giving an affirmative yes or no to an offer, the company will perceive that you're not taking them or the role on offer seriously.

The best way to avoid this situation is to manage their expectations ahead of time, as well as manage your timeline. If you're interviewing with three other companies and you've just received a request for a final interview, but you're just starting initial interviews with the others, you should do your best to speed up the other two and slow down the final interview. In doing so, you decrease the likelihood of an awkward or pressured situation where you have to make a decision to accept an offer quickly without seeing potential offers from your other options.

When negotiating your offers, keep the following best practices in mind:

Show up to the negotiation prepared. When I got my first job as a recruiter, I frankly had no idea what the average salaries were. I was just happy that a company wanted to hire me, but I did do basic research comparing base salaries, calculated my living costs, and had an open conversation about salary, asking for advice from the hiring manager. In retrospect, this might have put me in a weaker negotiating position, and I'd advise preparing a bit more than I did.

Knowing exactly what amount you should ask for not only helps you determine where to aim but also sets appropriate expectations with your potential new employer, often preventing you from wasting valuable time considering opportunities that cannot ultimately meet your financial needs. Don't be shy about making it known that you've come to this amount thoughtfully and have the data to back it.

Don't focus too much on the money. You are joining a company primarily because you fit the culture, believe in their mission, and feel like you can achieve your goals working there. Ultimately, if it only came down to money, then you'd jump ship for a slightly higher offer if you were to get it, which wouldn't be a great way to live life. Money is important; however, when you're in the "trenches" of recruitment taking late night calls with a hiring manager on the other side of the world and jumping around the city, you're not going to be daydreaming about your bonus all day. Who you work with, the clients, and the environment you're in are going to be greater motivators for your in the long run. With that in mind, don't get too focused on the money and use every piece of your offer as a bargaining chip, from your start date to your bonus, base, and any other perks you have. Evaluate what your priorities are.

It's all relative. While the difference between 3,500,000 and 4,500,000 is the same as 7,000,000 and 8,000,000 and only 1 million yen, it's going to make a relatively higher impact on your quality of life the lower your salary is. On the other hand, your standard of living isn't going to increase too much if it's from the 7-8 range. Don't get caught up in bickering over a couple of thousand dollars. If you're too pushy, the employer may get the impression that you're not that interested in the job (or only interested in the money) and withdraw the offer. I've seen this happen before, and I've actually done it myself when I became a hiring manager and was building up my team. Every interaction you have with the employer, from your first impression to the salary negotiation, is an opportunity for them to see how you communicate and work under pressure.

Leverage multiple offers. If you have received an offer from X recruitment company, it's in your best interested to tell Y recruitment company because you're then labeled as more "attractive" in their eyes and they'll likely speed up their decision-making process. At the end of the day, you want to have multiple options to select from, if possible. The benefit of having multiple offers is that you can use one offer as leverage against another. Perhaps if you're being offered 3.5 million by company X and 4 million by company Y, it's easy to take that information to company X, and, more often than not, they'll do their best to match the salary if they really want you. If you don't have multiple offers on the table, you can use statistics/salaries online to negotiate terms as mentioned above.

Be candid. Hiring managers don't like it when you change your mind or priorities on an offer halfway through the negotiation. It's a huge red flag and you run the risk of getting the offer pulled. Rather, they love to hear the words, "I'll accept the offer right away if I get X and Y." The company doesn't want to negotiate (unless they have to), so if you're bold and straightforward about what you want, you'll come off as confident and will make their lives and your life a lot simpler. Very plainly state your priorities and your terms, "I'm willing to start the job August 25th with a 4,000,000-yen base salary as per the industry standard."

Taxes

When you're budgeting for an apartment and living expenses, keep in mind the tax you'll have to pay. The first year living in Japan, you're exempt from paying "property tax." However, from your second year in Japan the local municipal office slaps a nice fat tax on you. The percentage depends on where you live, but it's usually 6% of your gross salary. By the way, as long as you're making under 20,000,000 Japanese yen, you're not required to file your own income taxes, and the company does it for you, which was a nice surprise to me. This tax calculator is the most accurate that I've found, and you can merely input your estimated earnings to calculate what your net earnings will be. http://japantaxcalculator.com

Independent vs. Permanent Employee

As a full-time employee in Japan ("seishain"), you're under an employment contract managed by HelloWork (the Japanese government's employment service office) and the Japanese government. You're usually paid once a month and have to pay deductions, which include pension, health insurance, and so forth. The majority of larger recruitment firms in Japan will hire you as a permanent employee, and that's how I started out. If it's your first time moving to Japan with little work experience, being hired as a permanent employee is the most straightforward and stable way to get a job without having to worry about other, often confusing and complicated, factors much.

It's also possible that you're hired as an "independent contractor" or "consultant" rather than a permanent employee. This has its pros and cons, and if you're already working in Japan, are familiar with the labor laws and have some financial stability, then this sort of contract can actually be quite beneficial. In Japanese, this contract type is referred to as "*Kojin Jigyou Nushi (*個人事業*)*. This gives you the status of independent contractor, but you don't have to start your own company. This is great because it means you can qualify for various benefits, but don't have to worry about registering as a business, submitting corporate taxes, and so forth.

The downside of the independent contractor status is that you lose most labor law protection rights, so beware; this isn't the most stable of routes, and it may make it harder to qualify for bank loans compared to a permanent status job. You also have to take care of all of your own taxes and pay a pension to yourself. That said, the benefit here is that almost *every single expense* you incur can be claimed as a business cost; at least in part. For example, a portion of your apartment, the cost of your computer, travel expenses, education fees, and so forth are all considered business expenses. Strictly speaking, it's a consulting agreement in which you're truly outsourced, meaning that you have no company email, business card, security pass, or login to any internal systems or tools.

CHAPTER 9

HOW TO MAKE THE BEST DECISION

When you have an offer in front of you, there are always at least two options. You can accept the offer, or you can reject the offer. More often than not, it's more complicated than that. There might be multiple offers on the table that are in different industries with different salaries and in different locations. You have to consider your living standards, long-term goals, your boss, your team, and possibly worry about a visa.

No matter what your decision, there will be a degree of uncertainty to it. Making a pros and cons list has traditionally been the easiest way to get close to the "best" decision, ever since Benjamin Franklin proposed it over 200 years ago. But the pros/cons list approach has its drawbacks. Namely, we're more likely to fall into what's called the *availability bias;* that is, we consider the options in front of us as they are, and start drawing conclusions based on that. For example, if the recruitment job has a high salary, big company, and great clients, this looks really good on paper. We might thus weigh these factors heavily, but what's easy to capture into words isn't necessarily the full picture.

You also wrote down, "Boss seems a bit strict." If we dug a bit deeper, perhaps we would identify a potentially bigger issue here. Using the same example, if you have a "bad feeling" about your boss to-be from the one meeting you had with him as well as from his own description of his management style, you shouldn't ignore your gut feelings. Your boss is the person you're going to sit next to every day, the person who will define the rules governing a large part of your working experience, or at the very least, the practical interpretation of those rules, and that will make or break your career. It would pay to examine this gut feeling closer by, for instance, having one more 1-hour meeting with your to-be boss to address any concerns you have. If the gut feeling doesn't go away, that's likely a bad sign.

This goes both ways. You can't only depend on your gut, and you can't only depend on the information you receive. Rather, you should be tuning into both to make an informed decision. The process looks like this:

> *Gather information about company* → *Assess information* → *Assess gut feelings* → *Follow up on gut feeling by gathering more information* → *Confirm/deny whether your gut feeling was accurate* → *Repeat process.*

Another example. Perhaps you're comparing two offers. Both have great teams, you like both bosses, and you're interested in the industry. The compensation is roughly the same. Both companies say they have a "discretionary" bonus system, but aren't totally clear on the details. They give you a rough figure, saying you can double your salary if you hit your targets. You have a feeling that that's probably not totally accurate. Also you feel this isn't enough information to make a decision. The best approach would be to ask deeper questions to both companies point blank. *Historically, how much money does an average new recruit make in my position? What is the actual salary? What is the highest/lowest they've made in their first year?* When company X gives you a straight answer with a specific example, but company Y doesn't tell you because it's "confidential" or "it depends," then you're better off placing your bets on company X.

I had several interviews with recruitment companies when I was getting into the industry. I had multiple offers on the table: an English teaching job (JET) and three separate offers from recruitment companies of different shapes and sizes. The decision wasn't easy, but in my personal case, I broke down my decision making process into several categories: my boss, pay, culture, industry, and team. At the time, salary and industry weren't so important to me, but when I compared the offers, I was looking at either pharmaceutical, industrial, or consumer technology. The latter appealed to me most.

But most of all, I gelled with everybody on the team, the CEO, and my future boss, so at the time, I used culture as the determining factor.

In many ways, I got lucky with my decision and things worked out well. In retrospect, though, I would have done a better analysis of *big company vs. small company*, which I basically overlooked. There was very little training provided in the job I choose to take. I could have experienced a more well defined training program at a larger firm, and then jumped to a smaller firm later (this is common). I was fortunate to have a good boss who was hands-on to help in training, but that's not something you should count on. Rather (now that you know some of the pros and cons from reading this book), you should confirm/double check your hunches during the interview process.

> *"Good decision-making starts with having multiple options available to you. Good decision-making involves collecting information that may contradict your initial opinions that you can sit at home with your pros and cons list and come up with a beautiful justification for whatever you wanted to do in the first place."*
> *-Chip and Dan Heath, Decisive*

Money is a short-term motivator

In the book *Drive*, author and psychologist Daniel Pink largely debunks the myth that we're motivated by extrinsic rewards, like paid time off or extra cash bonuses.

> *"When money is used as an external reward for some activity, the subjects lose intrinsic interest for the activity. Rewards can deliver a short term boost — just as a jolt of caffeine can keep you cranking for a few more hours. But the effect wears off — and worse, can reduce a person's longer-term motivation to continue the project."*

It reminds me of a particular instance in my previous recruitment job. We had a "2-day island getaway vacation" prize for hitting a certain sales target, but the employee who won didn't even want to go on the free trip because he didn't want to leave his dog at home (I'm sure he could have found a pet-sitter). He wasn't doing the job for silly prizes; he couldn't care less. He was doing the job because he legitimately enjoyed it.

Having purely monetary or reward driven factors as motivation for fulfilling a function affects the workplace in a number of ways. First, it's been shown that focusing on one extrinsic motivator like money narrows our focus and can lead to cutting corners, encouraging unethical behavior. It reminded me of some greedy merchants in Thailand who would inject extra water into watermelons to increase their weight, whereby they could charge more. Maybe the company overcharges and under delivers so that they can make an extra buck, or the sales guy decides to sacrifice quality so he can achieve a bigger bonus.

Second, when a manager gives a reward for performing

a task, he or she is basically signaling that the activity in itself isn't desirable and that they have to essentially pay you to do this "extra thing" (your job). The employee will then *expect* the reward in the future; so it better be there. The bigger problem here is that once the goal is achieved and the reward attained, what motivation does the employee have for exceeding their goal? Not much. Indeed, great customer service rarely comes from huge cash incentives but, instead, from a place of genuine empathy and attention to quality.

Of course, not all rewards are bad, and can actually help boost productivity and job satisfaction in very repetitive roles, short-term activities and as added motivation to achieve very specific goals. The idea is that if there's little intrinsic motivation to start out with, you can't really take it away by introducing a reward system for completing the job. For example, if you have to print and fold 1,000 letters — clearly a repetitive task — you'd probably get a good jolt of motivation from some cash reward. Arguably, you can also *develop* intrinsic motivation for menial tasks *without* extrinsic rewards, depending on your state of mind.

Nowadays, though, most of our jobs *aren't* about repetitively doing the same task every day; they require some creativity and collaboration. Recruitment requires you to juggle candidates, clients, and internal expectations on a daily basis. It has some repetitive aspects, but you're thinking on your feet and outside of the box on a daily basis.

Ultimately, everyone has different motivators that will also change throughout their lives and careers. Perhaps a recently married employee will value job security more than a recently graduated bachelor, who is more eager to take on overseas assignments. Some might value individual work more than team collaboration, a point you should take into consideration during team structuring. It's your job to find out what the motivators that you value are when considering a potential offer.

What are your motivators?

Our motivators change throughout our lives. When we're young, perhaps we're more open to taking risks, both in the type of job we do and our financial stability. Maybe we'll take a lower base salary with a higher bonus component because we don't mind eating cup noodles for a few weeks as we grind it out 24/7. This could quickly change if you have a family or big bills to pay; that guaranteed base salary is going to be a lot more reassuring when the baby's crying at 3am.

Personality and motivators are different; the former tends to stay static and the latter tends to change. It pays to assess both your own personality and motivators to get a rounded picture of what makes you tick, and then reassess them on at least a yearly basis. Myers-Briggs is the most famous personality test that you can take online. I've also pulled a list of top motivators from Attuned.ai, which is a corporate HR solution to assess employee motivation below, and a survey that I've taken myself as well (my top motivators were autonomy and progress.)

You might ask if there is a specific set of motivators that are common to great recruiters. The answer is, honestly, I'm not sure. There haven't been enough studies with a big enough data-set to come to a conclusive answer on this, but from experience, it really depends **on you and the company.** I've seen great recruiters with autonomy at the very top and the very bottom, with competition in the middle and the bottom. You may do great in one company but fail miserably in another. There doesn't seem to be a definitive pattern, but when I was at my previous company, *some* patterns specifically related to the culture we were in. People who had security and social relationships at the very top of their motivators tended to not do well in our firm. They tended to seek social validation and support, and they wanted to feel that the company as well as their salary/bonus were stable. Why didn't this work? Two reasons. The company was a startup recruitment firm, so, by definition, we weren't stable, and many of our employees were actually married and had little time for socializing. For someone who is motivated by security and social relationships, it's not hard to see why this didn't work out. On the other hand, that person could excel in a different environment. If they had gone to a larger recruitment firm that was more stable and perhaps had a larger group of people to socialize with, it's possible they would have thrived.

Or, for example, your top motivators could be *status and financial needs*. You would certainly thrive in an environment where you could get a big bonus and your boss gives you public praise and recognition of your successes on the job. However, if you were to place yourself in a company where you have a high base salary with little bonus earning potential and promotions are a long, drawn out process, then it is likely that you'll struggle to find job satisfaction there.

To assess your motivators, rank the following from one to ten, one being your top motivator now. You'll find that there are usually two or three that tend to be strongest.

1. Altruism
2. Autonomy
3. Competition
4. Feedback

5. Financial Needs
6. Innovation
7. Progress
8. Rationality
9. Security
10. Social Relationships
11. Status

Once you have these written down, you can assess the recruitment company (or other companies) that you're considering joining through the lens of your motivators. It's unlikely that a company is going to match up perfectly (nor could you likely assess it accurately enough to that degree). But, most importantly, you should assess whether or not the company meets your top three motivators. If it does, then you can likely thrive. The question to ask about the company is simply *how these motivators manifest*. I've listed some questions below that you should be asking about the company for you to consider in this process.

1. Altruism. *Is the bonus system team based? How do teams work together? Are they close-knit, or competitive?*
2. Autonomy. *What kind of management style does the boss have? Will I have to report everything to him on a daily basis? How flexible is he?*
3. Competition. *Is the recruitment company small with little desire for growth, like a lifestyle business? Or are they competing with other firms in the same sector?*

4. Feedback. *Do they have a culture of transparency? Will your boss give you frequent positive/negative feedback?*
5. Financial Needs. *What is their base, bonus system? How quickly can you get promoted? What are the historical results?*
6. Innovation
7. Progress. *How quickly can you get promoted? What are the historical results?*
8. Rationality. *Does their training, bonus system, strategy make sense to you? Do they use data in their decision making? How?*
9. Security. *Is the company stable? How long have they been around?*
10. Social Relationships. *What do employees do after work? Are there organized events? Do they have team incentives?*
11. Status. *How is the hierarchy structured in the company? How are decisions made? Are there incentive prizes and perks? What kind of clients will you have?*

Now, the business of motivation is complex, and there are going to be far more factors than just those listed above. In the perfect world, the employer would take a similar survey to determine what kind of people thrive in their environment and whether the results match up to your motivators. For now, you'll have to do this manually and spend time personally assessing each individual company/situation. While this requires you to ask a lot of questions and do more digging, it's worth the effort and you'll likely make a much better decision than most people who don't bother going into this level of detail.

If you want to take a more in-depth detailed report, you can visit the attuned website at https://www.attuned.ai/#product and sign up for a free trial.

The Yerkes-Dodson Sweet Spot

A principle in psychology called the Yerkes-Dodson law holds that stress (and associated arousal) makes a person more productive, but only up to a certain point. If you find a situation extremely tasking and exhausting you're not likely to function very well. On one hand, not *enough* stress/challenge results in an absence of motivation, and on the other too much stress puts you at risk of cardiovascular and immune problems, anxiety, and depression.

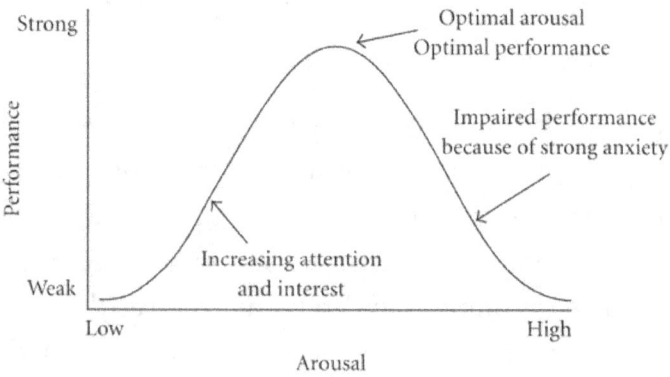

If your stress levels are in the optimum range, you're going to be more alert and attentive—"switched on." You'll also benefit from enhanced memory function and executive thinking capacities. To perform at your optimal level, you need to find the Yerkes-Dodson sweet spot. But how? We all have different levels of optimal stress and there could be any range of factors that influence this. Namely, if the motivators match up as discussed above, this is going to make the biggest impact.

There are also two other factors to consider:

#1. An authentic environment where you can express yourself. One study explored the role of authenticity, and found that employees who were more authentic at work were also more efficient, driven, and resilient.

#2. A growth mindset. Tested participants in a relevant study experienced symptoms of stress/anxiety. Naturally, certain symptoms made it harder for the participants to perform a cognitive task. However, when they were instructed to intentionally interpret their symptoms as signs of excitement (i.e., tricking themselves, in a sense), they were able to overcome the debilitating aspects of the stress and perform the task more effectively. In other words, your outlook on life can determine whether you think something is an exciting task to be tackled or a stressful/annoying activity to deal with.

When I joined the company, I knew that I had a lot to learn. It was my first job; I had only worn a suit once, and I had never properly learned how to use a calendar (I used to write my to do lists on my hand). There was so much to learn, and I accepted that as a simple fact. It also helped that I could look up to successful people around me. In other words, you've got to come in with a very high degree of humility, or else you'll get squashed.

In any case, before embarking on the journey to achieve your goal, whether that's joining a recruitment company or otherwise, ask yourself a few questions.

Will I be allowed to express my ideas and be authentic in this situation? If there's something blocking me, can I change it? Do I have an opportunity to get both positive and constructive feedback that helps me realize my strengths? Do I have a support network with people whom I can look up to and ask for help when necessary? Do I have a plan B and C? What's the worst that could happen? Could I get wiped out? And do I really want to do this?

You should be happy with your answers, and if you're not, then there might be *too* much risk. Keep in mind that if you're going to put yourself in a stressful environment that you want to overcome, you'll need to hit the sweet spot. That will be different for everyone and totally dependent on *your* situation. More often than not, though, you'll discover that taking the first leap into deep water is scary, but when we limit our options and are confronted with a tough but not impossible task, we're surprisingly good swimmers.

To summarize....

1. Don't just make a pros and cons list because it looks good. Follow your hunches and seek information to contradict yourself. Confirm whether those hunches are true or false.
2. It's not just about the money.
3. Self-assess your own motivators and determine how closely they fit with the company's operating methods.

CHAPTER 10

VOICES FROM RECRUITERS IN JAPAN

Romen Barua, Tokyo Supercars CEO / Konnex COO (recruitment blockchain startup)

What do you enjoy about recruitment?

"Creating value from customers and the recognition that you did a great job. I like the visible impact and result orientation also. Of course financial reward is nice too."

Benefits of work and life in Japan?

"A more abstract answer is that there are many benefits of being a foreigner here both socially and professionally. Generally there is less aggressive competition that's in your face and the pride and despair that you see in Western cultures as a result of success and failure is less prevalent here so being a risk taker alone in Japan can get you far I think just because you are a minority. You can also get caught in a trap,

> never never land and act like a 25-year-old indefinitely. It's dangerous because it is more acceptable to behave in a promiscuous manner here, which feeds a lot of foreigners here for life."

Anthony Beasley, Executive Recruiter at P.A.L KK

What do you enjoy about recruitment?

"It has not changed over time for me. I love this job because I can use over 90% of my abilities in this job. At most part, nothing holds me back. And I feel that the market needs me, which kicks in that 'being loved and needed by something' factor."

Biggest misconception new recruiters have?

"This is a sales job. And consultation can only be done with having a vast amount of data and trials, basically experiences. With this data, you can finally analyze. With the analysis, you can finally... confidently tell your candidates about what the current market is like, and give them your opinion about things."

Paul Roberts, Morgan McKinley, Manager, IT

What do you enjoy about recruitment?

"Successfully introducing someone to a role that changes that life significantly for the better. I found a job for the waiter at my yakitori restaurant once. He was a programmer during the day and working in the restaurant to pay for a English school. A month later he had doubled his salary after joining one of my clients, quit his night job, and was earning enough to marry his girlfriend. Great guy, we still keep in touch 17 years later."

Words of advice for new recruits?

"Be aware of all the pros and cons of the industry and why you're interested in getting into it. There is a ton of information online you can easily find. Research the companies you apply to thoroughly before interviews. Know your strengths and what you're bringing to the table. Ask good questions during interview, especially about the working culture, compensation scheme, and training."

Tetsu Nakamura, Recruiter @ Airbnb

Biggest differences between U.S. and Japan recruitment?

"In the United States, candidates focus a lot on career growth. That means that when I post a job, candidates actually apply. And when I talk to them about a job, they immediately ask what they can get out of it. American candidates want to know what's in it for them. In Japan, candidates often think about their family first. They are most concerned with job security. This makes them more passive and not want to be labeled as 'seeking new opportunities', so they don't. In general, I have to source more in Japan because it's harder to talk to candidates and get them to respond. And if they are looking for a job, they find them through agencies.... We reach out to a lot of Japanese candidates through Bizreach. It's known as the Japanese LinkedIn. But in general, even if you have a direct relationship with candidates, they don't tend to respond on these platforms. Our LinkedIn reply rate here is 3 to 5%, but in the U.S. it's often more than 10%."

Ben Yeargin, Owner of 550 Recruiting

What makes a great recruiter?

"I think there are a few qualities that top-notch recruiters all have in common: Open, Honest and Timely communication—-Top Recruiters don't beat around the bush. 1) Top Recruiters don't blow off their candidates when they realize they can't make a buck off of them. Top Recruiters don't wait 2 weeks after a hiring decision to let the rejected candidates know that they did not make the cut. 2) Top Recruiters realize that without the candidate they can't be successful and that the "brand" they show one candidate gets transferred, and impacts your future success. Make a candidate believe that you have their best interest in mind and they will tell two people. Blow one candidate off or make a candidate believe that you are just using them, or don't care about their future and they will tell 2,000 people."

Srikesh Chidambaram, Director at Excentive Japan

Challenges hiring in Japan?

"Sexism and ageism are rampant in Japan. There are lots of legal workarounds for it. You can be completely ageist in your hiring policies, for what's called succession planning here. And they base that on age. There are fantastic candidates out there who, once they hit a certain magical age, have a much harder time finding a job. Also, I've been told by employers a number of times that they would prefer a man in the job because they'll have to manage a team of people in their forties. I've been helping some companies resolve discriminatory practices: seeing if they have discrimination policies in effect; looking through their actual interview processes, how they are interviewing people, adding analytics to it; and educating."

Cameron Bret, Managing Director of Randstad Professionals

Your most important job as a leader in recruitment?

"As a leader, I think my most important job is hiring and retaining 'A' players. It's also one of the most difficult things to do in our industry. To retain 'A' players, I think you really need to know your people. You need to understand what motivates them and what engages them. In my experience, recruiters are economic animals, and an attractive and transparent compensation plan is important. As well, the guys on our team told us that training was important to them, so we've started to provide opportunities for overseas training programmes. We're also looking at how we can improve work–life balance. I think it starts with listening to people that you're managing and trying to find ways to keep them on board."

Casey Wahl, Founder and CEO of Wahl & Case

Advice for new recruiters?

"Do good and good will come back to you. Finish what you do, and do it with integrity - keep your word, and don't give in to short-term emotions. Too many people do that in business and it harms not only themselves, but the environment around them, breeding negativity. Emotions and behaviors are highly contagious. The more we can all act better in the work environment, the better it will become in reality."

Luke Palfrey, Recruiter at Enworld

"One of the reasons that recruiting is the second most popular choice for people without much experience is that you don't necessarily need any experience depending on the firm you're applying to. You could, of course, get into some more well-known firms if you have a good resume that shows you are very active and have been successful in your endeavors. The interviews can be very important as well, considering your personality and the way you sell yourself will be much more important than what's on your resume. The resume will just be what gets your foot in the door. There's something like over a thousand different recruiting firms in Japan so you'll have a good chance of getting into at least one if you can express your motivation and confidence."

CONCLUSION

New automation tools, motivational assessments, and big data HR analytics are redefining the way we are getting hired. Well, they're supposed to be anyways, but we're not quite there yet. Most people still find jobs through friends' recommendations and then buttoning up suit and tie to attend a good old- fashioned face-to-face interview. The change in the recruitment industry and hiring is going to be incremental, particularly in Japan where labor law hasn't changed in decades. But, in light of Japan's demographic challenges and labor shortage, there will have to be innovators who find a new approach to the issue of hiring and retaining good talent, at least, for the sake of the economy.

For the time being, recruitment remains important work and still retains its face to face element; the human aspect continues to be crucial. From a career perspective it's a lucrative, interesting, challenging, and rewarding job that's accessible to virtually anyone who is able to put in the hard work. While there are thousands of firms to choose from, which is a point I've pounded several times, it's unlikely that you'll fit many of them. A handful of companies will have a cultural fit with you, individually. I hope that I've given you the tools, ideas, and insights to better identify what that right fit looks like for you.

Of course, you have a lot of work to do ahead. I'm confident that if you're thorough, take time to prepare, and do your research, then you'll be successful.

Best of luck on your journey!

Misha Y.

One more thing...

Lastly, I provide a one-on-one consulting service that includes a 1-hour skype session with me. We can discuss your resume, feedback on your interview approach, advice on working in Japan, or any other questions you have. If you'd like to learn more, please visit the link here:

https://mishayurchenko.me/recruiter/

TOOLS AND RESOURCES

I've compiled a list of tools, websites, and links to help you in finding companies to apply and to better prepare for interviews.

You can also access this full list online. Visit this link to get the list from me: https://mishayurchenko.me/free-pdfs/

Resume Builder - https://www.gotresumebuilder.com/

Japanese Resume Builder

Recruitment Cold Calling Scripts

https://www.topechelon.com/blog/recruiter-training/8-scripts-that-recruiters-can-use-to-cold-call-candidates/

http://iheadhunter.blogspot.jp/2011/02/5-chalices-script-to-increase-candidate.html

http://www.recruitingblogs.com/profiles/blogs/headhunting-10-top-tips-for-making-more-successful-calls

http://theundercoverrecruiter.com/cold-calls/

https://www.slideshare.net/TopEchelon/cold-calling-scripts-for-recruiters

https://blog.pipedrive.com/2016/05/cold-calling-scripts/

http://recruitloop.com/blog/recruiter-tips-its-time-to-lose-the-script/

RescueTime (time saving app)

Quora - great, up to date Q&A w/ lots of job related and Japan specific advice https://www.quora.com/

Slideshare - great resource for interview and recruitment tips

https://www.slideshare.net/

Twitter for Job Hunting - https://jobmob.co.il/blog/beginners-guide-find-a-job-with-twitter/

Facebook for Job Hunting - https://www.forbes.com/sites/susanadams/2014/02/06/4-ways-to-use-facebook-to-find-a-job/#36cc63881fab

LinkedIn Hunter Chrome Extension - instead of paying for in mails to message on LinkedIn you can use this to phish for publicly listed emails, for free. https://chrome.google.com/webstore/detail/hunter/hgmhmanijnjhaffoampdlllchpolkdnj?hl=en

A list of recruitment companies in Japan:

https://www.angloinfo.com/tokyo/directory/tokyo-employment-agencies-south-tokyo-607

Business model of recruitment firms:

https://hr.ucr.edu/recruitment/guidelines/process.html

And http://recruitloop.com/blog/the-seven-stages-of-the-modern-recruiting-workflow/

Networking Events in Japan

https://www.doorkeeper.jp/events

https://www.meetup.com/cities/jp/tokyo/

https://businessinjapan.doorkeeper.jp/

http://www.cccj.or.jp/en/events

https://www.career-jpn.com/en

Free PDFs about the Japan Recruitment Market + Global Talent Market

Linkedin Global Recruitment rends 2016 **https://business.linkedin.com/content/dam/business/talent-solutions/global/en_us/c/pdfs/GRT16_GlobalRecruiting_100815.pdf**

Hays Global Skills Index **http://www.hays-index.com/countries/japan/**

The Talent Crunch:**http://page.ef.com/Talent-Crunch-Web.html**

W&C blog Japan**https://www.wahlandcase.com/news/**

Book Recommendations:

The Recruiter's Almanac of Scripts, Rebuttals and Closes

Search and Placement! A Handbook for Success

(revised)

Billing Power! The Recruiter's Guide to Peak Performance

How to Make People Like You in 90 Seconds or Less

The ONE Thing: The Surprisingly Simple Truth Behind Extraordinary Results

The Power of Habit: Why We Do What We Do in Life and Business

Good to Great: Why Some Companies Make the Leap...And Others Don't by Collins, Jim (2001) Hardcover

The Talent Code: Greatness Isn't Born. It's Grown. Here's How.

Headhunters (Vintage Crime/Black Lizard)

Guerrilla Marketing for Job Hunters 3.0: How to Stand Out from the Crowd and Tap Into the Hidden Job Market using Social Media and 999 other Tactics Today

Etiquette Guide to Japan: Know the Rules that Make the Difference! (Third Edition)

Who

Fanatical Prospecting: The Ultimate Guide to Opening Sales Conversations and Filling the Pipeline by Leveraging Social Selling, Telephone, Email, Text, and Cold Calling

Work Rules!: Insights from Inside Google That Will Transform How You Live and Lead

A Concise History of Japan (Cambridge Concise Histories)

STAR Interview

ACKNOWLEDGEMENTS

Several people contributed to making this book possible. I'm grateful to Romen Barua who believed in me enough to hire me in my first recruitment job and also added his valuable comments in the book. None of this would have been possible if Casey Wahl hadn't started W&C years ago, and I'm forever indebted. I'm also thankful to Paul Roberts, Anthony Beasel, Megumi Hirota, Matthew Marzi, and Cameron Bret for their feedback. Lastly, this book wouldn't have been possible without Rachel Joffe's editing and extensive edits/proofreading by Wayne Purdin. Thanks everyone!

MORE FROM MISHA

-A list of 50+ Book Recommendations: https://mishayurchenko.me/misha-recommends/

-Misha's Blog and Weekly Newsletter: http://mishayurchenko.me/

-Books: https://mishayurchenko.me/mybooks/

www.ingramcontent.com/pod-product-compliance
Lightning Source LLC
Chambersburg PA
CBHW071500220526
45472CB00003B/866